REMEMBRANCE ROAD

A Canadian photographer's journey through European battlefields

Justine MacDonald

www.sspub.ca

Copyright © 2018 Justine MacDonald

All rights reserved. No part of this book may be reproduced or transmitted in any form or by any means, electronic or mechanical, including photocopying, or by an information storage or retrieval system without permission in writing from the publisher.

SSP Publications recognizes the support of the Province of Nova Scotia. We are pleased to work in partnership with the Department of Communities, Culture and Heritage to develop and promote our cultural resources for all Nova Scotians.

Library and Archives Canada Cataloguing in Publication

MacDonald, Justine, 1978-, author, photographer
    Remembrance road : a Canadian photographer's journey through European battlefields / Justine MacDonald.

ISBN 978-0-9868733-9-3 (softcover)

    1. MacDonald, Justine, 1978- --Travel--Europe, Western.
2. Photographers--Travel--Europe, Western. 3. World War, 1939-1945--Battlefields--Europe, Western--Pictorial works.
4. World War, 1939-1945--Europe, Western--Pictorial works.
5. Europe, Western--Description and travel. I. Title.

D967.M332018   914.04'5612   C2018-905612-6

BISAC   HIS027050
Design: Graphic Detail
Printed in Canada

Box 2472, Halifax, NS, B3J 3E4 Canada
www.sspub.ca
sspub@hotmail.com

Front cover: The door into the remining gas chamber at Auschwitz I. (2017)

Back cover: Trenches at Hill 62, Mount Sorrel (2017)

Facing page: The Vimy 100 ceremony included music, song and interpretive dance representing Canada's English, First Nations and French populations. (2017)

The Poppy Design is a registered trademark of The Royal Canadian Legion, Dominion Command and is used under licence.

Dedication

To my family for all the opportunities they have given me, and to all those who have sacrificed in the service of their country in foreign lands.

Lest we forget.

Canadian flags left along Juno Beach, Normandy, France. (2017)

*They shall grow not old,
as we that are left grow old:
Age shall not weary them,
nor the years condemn.
At the going down of the sun
and in the morning
We will remember them.*[1]

Poppies, ANZAC Cove, Gallipoli, Turkey. (2015)

---

[1] Excerpt from *For the Fallen*, Binyon, L., as cited on Veterans Affairs Canada. (2017). *A guide to commemorative services*. Retrieved from http://www.veterans.gc.ca/eng/remembrance/get-involved/remembrance-day/guide-to-commemorative-services#act.

Contents

Foreword	7
Introduction	9
PART I: THE WAR TO END ALL WARS	19
The Gallipoli Campaign	25
A Brief History of the Gallipoli Campaign	26
My Tour of the Gallipoli Battlefields: Helles Tour	29
My Tour of the Gallipoli Battlefields: ANZAC Tour	38
The Newfoundlanders in Beaumont-Hamel	49
Beaumont-Hamel National Historic Site of Canada	50
Canadians at Vimy Ridge	57
Fields in Flanders	71
The First Battle of Ypres	72
The Second Battle of Ypres	72
The Battle of Passchendaele	74
Menin Gate	76
Tyne Cot Cemetery	79
Essex Farm	80
Sanctuary Wood	84
PART II: WORLD WAR II	91
D-Day	103
Juno Beach	107
Gold Beach	112
The Holocaust	117
Remembering the Dead	133
Appendix One - Relevant Dates	149
Bibliography and Resources	150
Acknowledgements	152
About the Author	155

Foreword

I am a travel photographer. I do not think of my photographs as photojournalism, however, but as art. As such, I have no problem editing my photographs to achieve the specific look or feel I want to portray in the image.

While I do have a love of history, and specifically military history, I am not a historian – not even an armchair one. I own a small library of military history books and I am always on the search for fresh audio and video content. I focus more on the stories and themes of what I read, never having been good at remembering specific facts and figures. These are important though, so I have included a brief history of World War I and World War II as they relate to these essays and have done my best to ensure the information is accurate.

Morning shoot in the Sahara Desert, Morocco. (2015)

Finally, I want to stress that these are my interpretations and impressions of the history and the sites, as we approach the centenary of the end of World War I. I encourage you to do your own research and to visit these sites for yourself, if possible, to develop your own impressions. I would love for you to share your stories with me and, more importantly, share those stories with your community.

~ Justine

31-01-2018

Facing page: Skeletons of D-Day remain on Gold Beach – one of Britain's two landing beaches on 6 June, 1944. (2017)

Introduction The Making of a Travel Photographer

To open this book, I chose to include the Act of Remembrance.[2] It is a pledge recited each Remembrance Day and has been at the forefront of my mind for the last few years. It led me on a journey I could not have anticipated when, looking up at the towering pylons of the Vimy Memorial in France, twenty years ago, I pledged to return for the centenary of the battle in 2017.

The first time I remember thinking that being in the military was more than just a job my dad did, was when I came across a book in our home library. I do not remember how old I was the first time I saw it. It was a home-made book with a hard, red cover decorated with a collage of pictures. My dad wrote the book about his time in Cyprus, when he served in the Canadian Army as part of the United Nations forces deployed to the country after the Turkish invasion of 1974. I have not seen that book in years, and I cannot remember what exactly he wrote about, but I remember it made things a bit more real for me; it was my first introduction to military history.

The First Camera

I was a military brat and we lived on a military base in Alberta. My dad was in the Canadian Army in 1975, when he met my British mother who had been a member of the Women's Royal Air Force. They met when they were both serving in Cyprus.

We lived in Alberta until I was sixteen and I loved it there. With lots of imagination and an endless forest (at least in the explorations of a child), there was no shortage of things to do. I think I was about eight or nine when I got my first real camera – a skinny little 110mm point-and-shoot. After I got the camera, it came with me on those adventures. I remember racing around the base on my bicycle

Facing page: Sunset over the fields near Geilenkirchen, Germany, on the Siegfried Line in World War Two and, more recently, my home for five years. (2017)

---

[2] The pledge is an excerpt from the poem *For the Fallen* by Laurence Binyon (Public Domain material). You can find the pledge, along with more information on Remembrance Day services, on the Veterans Affairs Canada website: veterans.gc.ca.

with the camera in my pocket. Back then, most of my photos were of my friends. The camera soon succumbed to the rough treatment of a young, active girl.

The Traveller

As I got older, repetition improved my photography (even if it was unintentional) and my adventures started taking me farther afield – England to visit family and a trip with my Pathfinder group to the Rocky Mountains. I was no stranger to travelling, even if we did not do it very often. I had my first passport when I was a year old, so my mum could take me home to meet her family.

My grandparents seemed to enjoy travelling, whether it was just going camping or travelling around the world to visit my mum. My grandmother documented these trips with a travel journal. That sounded like a great idea, but it also sounded like a lot of work. Writing is hard, especially after a long day of adventures. Taking pictures sounded a lot easier; they were worth a thousand words after all. That was around the time my photos started to feature less people and more places and things as I used the medium to document the world around me.

In 1994, we moved to Winnipeg. One summer I embarked on another trip to England to visit family and explore historic sites in their region. My dad took me to the base and put me on a C-130 Hercules, a military transport aircraft, bound for England where I met up with my family and spent a couple of weeks with my grandparents before school started.

Learning about History

It was not my first time on a military aircraft. All the bases we were posted to organized 'family days'. We could go on the aircraft and have tours of the area. I saw the scenery of Alberta from a helicopter and checked out Christmas lights above Winnipeg in the Hercules.

The flights on this trip would be my longest on the aircraft. I was seventeen and, sitting in the web seats, it was the first time I had the sense of being somewhere important, even if I think my dad might have scoffed at that.

The C-130 Hercules is used by the Royal Canadian Air Force for search and rescue, supply and equipment transport, troop movement and air-to-air refuelling.[3] I only ever got the funny or interesting stories from my dad about his time on the Hercules, but I knew he and the rest of his crew were doing more than just supplying embassies, giving tours to dignitaries and being a private airline to military families.

There were only a few people on each of the flights it took to reach England. I looked around the empty space and imagined it full of vehicles and equipment; the line of web seats used by men in uniform deploying to Bosnia, or Rwanda, or Croatia, or any number of other conflict zones we were involved in at the time. I could also envision military personnel and civilians alike saved in search and rescue operations. I remember my dad telling me once, when I asked, that his aircraft was shot at but reassuring me that they were just warning shots. I wondered how much of a 'warning' they were truly given.

That flight and finding dad's Cyprus book were the moments that made the military and its importance real to me, which is ironic considering I grew up surrounded by uniforms and the sounds of fighter jets. I started to pay more attention. During parties and dinners, I may have been sitting with the women and children, but I kept an ear on the guys talking shop.

It made me think more about the context of the places I visited. That is something, all these years later, that I stress the importance of whenever I give workshops and lectures on travel and photography.

What is this thing or place used for? Who lived and died here? What cries and laughter have been heard here? What secrets do the walls, or dirt, or water keep? What are the stories that did not make it into the books and what could we learn from them if we knew them? Only by thinking about these questions can we appreciate where we are and who we are meeting.

Web seats on a Hercules display aircraft in Greenwood, Nova Scotia. (2016)

---

[3] Royal Canadian Air Force. (2017). *CC-130 Hercules*. Retrieved from http://www.rcaf-arc.forces.gc.ca/en/aircraft-current/cc-130.page

I believe it is the reason that, as I grew into being a photographer, I was drawn to those clichéd photographs of derelict buildings or decaying barns. I think it may be why I enjoy finding and photographing graffiti on buildings and bridges – it is a record of someone being there and the art they leave behind often says more than their words might if I were to meet them. Perhaps that is why I was drawn to history and archaeology in university, even if I did not pursue these fields. Although, seeing where my photography has led me, perhaps I ended up there in the end. I just took the scenic route.

The scenic routes are always the best.

Moving Overseas

In 1996, we were planning a trip to Disneyworld in Florida. I remember not being all that interested in it. At eighteen, I was probably at that age where Disney was not cool. For some reason, my parents left it to me to plan the road trip (I ended up being the family travel agent from that point forward). I planned a route that would lead down the east coast of the United States through important sites of the American Civil War. I thought that would be much more interesting, not to mention educational, for my brother and I, than Disney.

One day, a few months into this planning, dad came home with orders. We were about to embark on a much bigger adventure - we were moving to Germany.

On the coldest night in Winnipeg so far that year, we left our shovel in the snow bank at the end of what was no longer our driveway and did not look back until we had to return almost five years later. We did not waste a second of our time in Germany. Within our first month in Europe, my mother and I were on a train to England.

Our new house was just outside of Geilenkirchen, near the Dutch border. In World War II, it was on the Siegfried Line, protecting Germany from the Allies. In November 1944, the line was tested when American and British forces chose this point to break through after D-Day on the way to Berlin.[4] The Americans advanced right down my street. After a hard battle in a wet, muddy German winter, the Allies managed to take the town, but made no further progress.[5]

Whenever we could, we packed up a picnic and took a day trip somewhere as a family. Usually we had a specific destination in mind, but sometimes we just followed the roads where they lead us and that so often led to the most interesting adventures. We saw Neander, Hamlin, Luxembourg, markets and more, including one town's seven-hundredth birthday celebration. We took big trips too – Scotland, Cyprus, Bavaria. The Canadian Forces Morale and Welfare Services planned lots of excursions and trips and we took advantage of those as well – travelling to Hungary, Sweden, Prague and even a rock concert.

We saw the centuries-old Scottish battlefields of Culloden (1745) and Bannockburn, near Stirling (1314); and the Napoleonic battlefield of Waterloo (1815). We saw evidence of more recent conflicts in the middle east – sitting in a tour bus, escorted by police, as we drove through the West Bank on the way to Bethlehem and then on to Jerusalem. In the Cypriot capitol of Nicosia, the Green Line continues to separate the Turks from the Greeks.

We heard stories from our neighbour who escaped Eastern Germany and comments from her husband that made us think he was more than likely a once-proud member of the Hitler Youth, still holding onto at least some of those ideals.

We observed Remembrance Day at the Groesbeek War Cemetery in The Netherlands, surrounded by the graves of a small number of the fallen whom we remembered during the service. Twice we travelled to Nijmegen, also in The Netherlands, to show our support to our military, along with service members from Britain, Germany and other countries, as they approached the end of the Nijmegen

Brunssum War Cemetery, The Netherlands. 328 British casualties (one unidentified and most from the Battle of Geilenkirchen), are buried here.[6] (2017)

---

[4] Ford, K. (1994). *Assault on Germany: The battle for Geilenkirchen*. Southampton, England: Valda Books, pp. 11-12.
[5] Ibid, p. 179.
[6] Commonwealth War Graves Commission. (n.d.). *Cemetery*. Retrieved from https://www.cwgc.org/find-a-cemetery/cemetery/2059100/brunssum-war-cemetery/

View from a checkpoint on the Green Line in Nicosia, Cyprus. (1998)

Victory March. This annual march followed the path of the liberation of The Netherlands near the end of World War II. We cheered and waved flags; children gave the men and women high fives and flowers. Today, if you see small groups of soldiers marching around your town with their packs on in the late spring or early summer, they may be preparing for the Nijmegen March.

After years of visiting random military sites on various excursions, we had just six months left in Europe. It was time to make a trip to the major battlefields in our region – Normandy, Dieppe, Flanders. It was a chance to reflect not only on the sacrifices made by those who fought and died on these battlefields and beaches, but also on our time in Europe.

We returned to Canada in 2001, moving into our house on 9/11 and the start of a new war. Again, our Canadian service members were deployed to fight a war in foreign lands. From 2002 to 2011,

Canada lost 158 men and women in Afghanistan.[9] Hundreds would gather along the Highway of Heroes in Ontario to pay their respects to the fallen being repatriated to Canada. Every loss, every sacrifice of our more recent veterans matters. They should not be forgotten when we remember those who have fought in defence of Canada.

Groesbeek Canadian War Cemetery, The Netherlands. The cemetery contains 2,619 World War II burials (21 unidentified)[7] and a memorial etched with the names of another 1,016 who fell and have no known graves. Most of the fallen in this cemetery died in the Battle of the Rhineland in the winter of 1945.[8] (1999)

But in World War I and Two, so many people died they could not be brought home. 158 dead would have been a 'good' day at Vimy, or the Somme, or the beaches of Normandy. Canada alone lost more than 66,000 lives in the four years of World War I[10] and 45,000 in the six-year long World War II[11]. Those numbers, and the images from the battlefields, remained in my mind and would not leave. I returned to them from time to time in the years after returning to Canada and told anyone who would listen about my experiences.

I would not visit a battlefield again until 2015, when I travelled to the World War I landing beaches and battlefields of Gallipoli, Turkey, where the Australian and New Zealand Army Corps[12] (ANZAC), British, French and Newfoundland forces were trapped for months between the Ottoman Empire and the sea after attempting to open up a route through the Dardanelles Straits to the Black Sea.[13]

---

[7] Commonwealth War Graves Commission. (n.d.). *Cemetery*. Retrieved from https://www.cwgc.org/find-a-cemetery/cemetery/2063900/groesbeek-canadian-war-cemetery/
[8] Commonwealth War Graves Commission. (n.d.). *Cemetery*. Retrieved from https://www.cwgc.org/find-a-cemetery/cemetery/2063700/groesbeek-memorial/
[9] Veterans Affairs Canada. (n.d.). *Fallen Canadian Armed Forces*. Retrieved from http://www.veterans.gc.ca/eng/remembrance/history/canadian-armed-forces/afghanistan-remembered/fallen
[10] Veterans Affairs Canada. (2017). *The First World War*. Retrieved from http://www.veterans.gc.ca/eng/remembrance/history/first-world-war
[11] Veterans Affairs Canada. (2017). *The Second World War*. Retrieved from http://www.veterans.gc.ca/eng/remembrance/history/second-world-war
[12] *Corps* - Each of a country's Army Groups is made up of at least one Corps, which in turn is made up of two or more divisions.
[13] Uttridge, S., & Catton, C. (2014). *The encyclopedia of warfare*. London: Amber Books, pp. 788-9.

Returning to the Battlefields

In 2017, the year of Canada's 150th birthday, I fulfilled that 1998 promise to myself and returned to the battlefields of Western Europe to attend a ceremony marking the centenary of the Battle of Vimy Ridge. I travelled with my aunt and we chose a tour with GoAhead Tours for most of the trip. That tour company is a division of Education First (EF) – frequently used by schools and other youth organizations for educational travel. Altogether, EF was responsible for over a third of the 25,000 attendees at the ceremony in France on 9 April 2017. We were all issued red jackets to wear at the ceremony and my aunt and I wore ours for most of the trip.

In addition to the Vimy 100 Ceremony, we travelled from Paris to Amsterdam, visiting important Canadian and British battlefields

A headstone in the Bergen-op-Zoom Canadian War Cemetery, The Netherlands. It contains 1,119 burials (31 unidentified).[14] (2017)

[14] Commonwealth War Graves Commission. (n.d.). *Cemetery.* Retrieved from https://www.cwgc.org/find-a-cemetery/cemetery/2061700/bergen-op-zoom-canadian-war-cemetery/

and landing beaches along the way. While these were all new experiences for my aunt, many of the sites, like Normandy and Dieppe, I had visited before. Others, such as the battlefield of The Somme, were new for me as well. After our ten day tour, we rented a car and travelled through The Netherlands to Flanders before flying to Poland to visit the infamous Auschwitz concentration camp.

Remembrance Road

The Vimy 100 Ceremony was just one reason for this trip. It was important, I felt, to return to the battlefields. I wanted to learn more, reflect more. I wanted to photograph the battlefields in a way that I hoped would do the sites justice. Most of all, I wanted to come back home and share the experience with my community, to try and help those who will never make it to the battlefields understand the scale of the conflicts and to stress the importance of never forgetting. I wanted to help others remember to remember.

How would I do that? I am no expert on the subject. I am not in the military and have no desire to be. I am just a girl with a camera who likes to spend all her money (and a lot of money she does not have) travelling around the world taking photographs that sometimes surprise her and turn out well. Who did I think I was to do this? But maybe… maybe I could get one more person to remember.

After returning from the trip, I started work on a photographic and historical exhibit. It ran for three months in the fall of 2017 at the Kings County Museum in Kentville, Nova Scotia, with a smaller photographic exhibit hosted in Halifax during the first half of November. I also presented eight lectures about my trip. This collection of essays and photographs is an extension of that project.

I called it *Remembrance Road* and it was the culmination of almost forty years of travel, photography and experiences growing up in a military family, mixed with my desire to ensure we remember the past as we move into the future.

Part I

The War to End all Wars   World War I | 1914 – 1918

There have not been many times in history when a single bullet could change the world so drastically, and for so long, as one did in the summer of 1914. One could argue that the impact of that bullet can still be felt today.

On 28 June 1914, Archduke Francis Ferdinand and his wife were assassinated during an appearance in Sarajevo.[15] At the time, the nations of Europe were tied together through a network of treaties and protection pacts. It caused the countries to fall one-by-one as war-like dominoes.

With Germany's support, Austria-Hungary declared war on Serbia in response to the assassination. Russia sided with the Serbians and the French were allies with Russia. It created a two-front war for Germany. They needed to strike quickly at France through Belgium, so they could focus on Russia before that country fully mobilized. Neutral Belgium refused to grant Germany passage.[16] Germany took their passage by force and Ypres, in the Flanders region of Belgium, became the epicentre for the Western Front.[17] By 1915, there were eight hundred kilometres of trenches stretching through Western Europe from the North Sea to the Swiss border.[18]

The German invasion of Belgium brought Britain into the war on 4 August 1914 and consequently, the British colonies around the world. Canada had no choice but to follow. At the time, we were a country of just eight million people. By the end of the war, we had sent four full divisions and 619,636 men to fight in Europe. Our forces were decimated, with 66,655 killed in action or dying of wounds or disease.[19] Atlantic Canada played a big part in the war.

Facing page: This Canadian monument is nestled in a peaceful enclosure outside the Belgian village of St. Julien. *The Brooding Soldier* stands in a pillar of stone "gas", leaning on his upturned rifle, mourning his fallen comrades. (2017)

---

[15] McKay, J. P., Buckler, J., & Hill, B. D. (2001). *A history of Western society*. Boston: Houghton Mifflin, p. 895.
[16] Ibid, p. 896.
[17] Humphreys, E. (2014). *Great Canadian battles*. London, United Kingdom: Arcturus, p. 288.
[18] Black, D., & Boileau, J. (2015). *Old enough to fight: Canada's boy soldiers in the First World War*. Toronto: James Lorimer & Company, p. 84.
[19] Ibid, p. 285.

Camp Aldershot, near Kentville, Nova Scotia, was the largest training centre in Eastern Canada housing 7,000 men during its peak in 1916.[20] The 85th Battalion, from Nova Scotia, secured one of the final objectives in the Battle of Vimy Ridge. The Royal Newfoundland Regiment struggled through the long campaign in Gallipoli, only to be almost wiped out at The Somme.

In 1915, a German submarine sank the British passenger liner *Lusitania*. Among the thousand plus lives lost were 139 Americans. The Germans, fearing the United States would join the war if more of its citizens were caught in the crossfire, pulled back on submarine warfare. By 1917, they believed the defeat of Britain would be complete before the United States could mobilize, much like their decision to try and reach France before the Russians could mobilize at the opening of the war.[21] Submarine warfare resumed and America entered the war.

As for the Russians, growing tensions at home, eventually leading to full revolution, forced the nation to withdraw from the war in 1918, allowing Germany to focus all its attention on the Western Front. Fighting the two-front war for so long, however, had worn them out and though inexperienced, the United States brought an entire nation of fresh troops and increased supplies to add to those of the British and French armies.[22] In what had become a war of attrition, the numbers simply won the day for the Allies.

Germany surrendered, without the Allies setting foot on German soil, near the end of the year, with the armistice coming into effect at 11:11 a.m. on 11 November 1918.[23] It is thought that Port Williams, Nova Scotia native Private George Lawrence Price was the last Canadian killed in the war – at 10:58 a.m., just a few minutes before the armistice. He is buried in Belgium.[24] The resulting peace talks opened the following January at the Palace

---

[20] Tennyson, B. D. (2017). *Nova Scotia at War, 1914-1919*. Toronto: Nimbus Publishing, Limited, p. 176.
[21] McKay, J. P., Buckler, J., & Hill, B. D. (2001). *A history of Western society*. Boston: Houghton Mifflin, p. 904.
[22] Ibid, p. 916.
[23] Ibid.
[24] Commonwealth War Graves Commission. (n.d.). *Casualty*. Retrieved from https://www.cwgc.org/find-war-dead/casualty/894901/price,-george-lawrence/

of Versailles, near Paris. The Treaty of Versailles was signed in the famous hall of mirrors on 28 June 1919.[25]

The Allies came to this new war the same way they had come to older ones. They brought felt hats, rifles and bayonets and ceremonial swords while the Germans brought machine guns and chlorine gas. Shelling was intense, often constant, and certainly long-lasting. The war was one of trenches, attrition and almost static front lines. It was also one of continuous innovation. By 1917, the Allies had learned the rules of this new war and were beginning to change their course.

Such intense, prolonged conditions were new and the term shell-shock entered our vocabulary. The cases and symptoms grew in number and intensity and were often not taken seriously – those afflicted were called cowards or weak, or accused of faking illness. Unfortunately, these sentiments have not completely disappeared from today's militaries. Known today as post-traumatic stress disorder, the condition was not new. In his book *Odysseus in America*, Jonathan Shay suggests there is written evidence of the condition dating as far back as Homer's epic *The Odyssey*.[26]

The war even touched us here on Canadian shores in December 1917, when two supply ships collided in Halifax Harbour to create one of the worst man-made explosions in history.[27]

Looking north toward Pier 8 from Hillis foundry after great explosion, Halifax, Dec. 6, 1917

Nova Scota Archives - Halifax explosion

---

[25] McKay, J. P., Buckler, J., & Hill, B. D. (2001). *A history of Western society*. Boston: Houghton Mifflin, p. 917.
[26] Shay, J. (2002). *Odysseus in America: Combat trauma and the trials of homecoming*. New York: Scribner.
[27] National Post. (2017). *Halifax Explosion: A look at the largest man-made explosion in history before Hiroshima*. Retrieved from http://nationalpost.com/news/canada/halifax-explosion-a-look-at-the-largest-man-made-explosion-in-history-before-hiroshima

War was no longer a gentlemanly, honourable sport, even if the old guard seemed unwilling to acknowledge the change. The younger recruits, new to the military and to war – guys living in the trenches and seeing the tremendous loss of life as year after year went by, had a different view of the war. We can see those different viewpoints by looking at their memoirs, art and poetry.

John McCrae, a veteran of the Second Boer War, wrote *In Flanders Fields* after the 1915 death of his friend in Flanders. It urges the reader to take up the fight from those who have fallen, dying honourably for their country. Wilfred Owen arrived on the front lines in 1916 in his early twenties and soon realized the war was not as promised. His poem, *Dulce et Decorum Est,* describes the horrors of the war in vivid detail and urges us to realize that there is nothing sweet or honourable about dying for one's country, especially not in the trenches of World War I. As with most debates, the truth lies probably somewhere in the middle.

Lt.-Col. John McCrae and his dog Bonneau, ca. 1914

Library and Archives Canada/Oskar Klotz fonds/c046284

The War to End all Wars

Excerpt from *In Flanders Fields*

Take up our quarrel with the foe!
To you from failing hands we throw
The torch; be yours to hold it high!
If ye break faith with us who die
We shall not sleep, though poppies grow
In Flanders fields.

Excerpt from *Dulce et Decorum Est*

If in some smothering dreams you too could pace
Behind the wagon that we flung him in,
And watch the white eyes writhing in his face,
His hanging face, like a devil's sick of sin;
If you could hear, at every jolt, the blood
Come gargling from the froth-corrupted lungs,
Obscene as cancer, bitter as the cud
Of vile, incurable sores on innocent tongues,—
My friend, you would not tell with such high zest
To children ardent for some desperate glory,
The old Lie: Dulce et decorum est
Pro patria mori.

Map showing major World War One sites visited

The Gallipoli Campaign   Gallipoli, Turkey | February 1915 – January 1916

Here is a confession: before 2015, I had no idea that the World War I battlefields of Gallipoli and the ruins of ancient Troy were both in Turkey. My memory is pretty vague on where I thought they were. I thought Gallipoli was perhaps in Libya, somewhere around Tripoli, probably. They are places that sound the same, so of course they would be right next to each other, like Mexico and Morocco. At least I had the right area of the world. All I knew about Troy was that it was not in Greece. I figured it was probably in Iraq or Iran or one of those cradle-of-civilization countries near the Euphrates.

Of course there are many other people who also have no idea where these places are, if they've heard of them at all. Given my 'historic' interests, however, I feel like I should have known.

One day, after signing up for a photography workshop and tour in Turkey, the organizer and photo leader, Shari, posted a link on her Facebook page about the 'Gallipoli Artist' in the context of the Turkey trip. I was checking Facebook at work and immediately started the search to see if there were tours to the battlefields. Through that search I learned that not only was Troy also in Turkey, it was practically in the same area. That makes sense, given the strategic importance of the Gallipoli peninsula.

With Shari's help, along with the Gallipoli Artist himself, Roachie, who is not only a wonderful artist but a tour operator, I booked a three day excursion to visit the battlefields.

I found this weekend of tours to be very different from my visits to the battlefields in Western Europe. To start, I had never had a guide before (although my father had always done a pretty good job with his historical information) or specifically researched an area before visiting. It was always just me and my family and whatever knowledge we had of the battle or area that we picked up along the way. Having guides, especially ones native to the area, was a great experience. They were all extremely knowledgeable and provided a

Facing page: Turkish 57th Regiment Memorial and symbolic cemetery in the ANZAC sector. (2015)

KilitBahir Fortifications at the Dardanelles Narrows, Gallipoli, Turkey. (2015)

different perspective of these battlefields, where the British Empire had invaded their homeland.

I saw so much in such a short period of time and documented what I saw with some amazing photographs.

A Brief History of the Gallipoli Campaign

After the Ottoman Empire (now Turkey) sided with Germany, Britain planned a naval attack to break through the waterways running across the country to link up with its Russian allies. To do so, they had to face three groups of fortifications along the Dardanelles Strait, including seventy-two guns at its narrowest point. There were also torpedo tubes from the coast, mines in the waterways, and Mother Nature herself (in the form of strong currents) to contend with. The expected naval success did not materialize and a land invasion was launched on 25 April 1915.[28]

---

[28] Nicholson, G. W. L. (2007). *The fighting Newfoundlander.* Montréal, Québec: McGill-Queen's University Press, pp. 166-7.

The Gallipoli Campaign

A view of the Gallipoli landing beaches, in the ANZAC region, from the Chunuk Bair memorial and cemetery. (2015)

British forces invaded an area defended by an army made up of natives to the area, but also people from across the vast Ottoman Empire, supported by Austria-Hungary and the German Empire. For the most part, each allied contingent controlled a different sector in the region. The Newfoundlanders (not a part of Canada until after World War II) were in Suvla, while the French settled at the south of the peninsula. British and ANZAC forces occupied the area in between.

Poor planning, leadership and logistics created a standstill. The two armies slogged away for almost a year, gaining little or no land in either direction until, after a change in command, the British staged a peaceful retreat.

The Gallipoli Campaign was the Newfoundland Regiment's first experience with battle in World War I. The fresh, untested troops entered the fray late in the campaign. After a year of travelling, training and preparing in both England and Alexandria, Egypt, 1,076 Newfoundlanders landed at Suvla Bay[29] under the cover of darkness. Their first impressions of war were more than likely the night sky lighting up with artillery fire, filled with the sounds of shelling from both sides and, when the landing crafts' engines stopped, rifle fire[30]. They landed on 20 September 1915 and suffered fifteen casualties[31] on their first day in the region; their first fatality came two days later. The Regiment did not even enter the front lines until 30 September.[32]

As part of the evacuation of the Suvla and ANZAC sectors, the Newfoundland Regiment withdrew with zero casualties on the night of 18 December, only to be redeployed to support the British in the Helles region. The final withdrawal of Allied forces came on the night of 8/9 January 1916. Some accounts say they managed the retreat in secret. Others say their opponents, just as tired of the fighting, allowed them to go.

---

[29] Nicholson, G. W. L. (2007). *The fighting Newfoundlander.* Montréal, Québec: McGill-Queen's University Press, p. 157.
[30] Ibid, p. 169.
[31] The term "casualties" includes those killed, wounded and missing.
[32] Nicholson, G. W. L. (2007). *The fighting Newfoundlander.* Montréal, Québec: McGill-Queen's University Press, pp. 170-2.

By the time they sailed away from the coast of Gallipoli, the Newfoundlanders were just 400 strong with most of their losses due to disease and ravages of the elements rather than fighting.[33]

My Tour of the Gallipoli Battlefields

I arrived in Turkey on the night of 25 September 2015. After sleeping at the Istanbul airport that night, I boarded a bus for the four hour drive to Ecebat, near Çanakkale on the Gallipoli peninsula. We arrived in time for lunch at a local restaurant before I was whisked away for a tour of the ruins of Troy. It wasn't until the next day that I began to explore the Gallipoli battlefields. With only a couple of days in the area, however, I was unable to visit the Suvla sector.

Helles Tour

According to my knowledgeable Turkish guides, much of the infrastructure and Turkish memorials in the area were created in the previous ten years or so, perhaps in preparation for the 90th and 100th anniversaries of the campaign. The region is a popular destination for Australians and New Zealanders on ANZAC Day (25 April).

We stopped at many spots throughout the region, starting with one of the fortifications guarding the Dardanelles Narrows. Kilitbahir features the remnants of the fort as well as gun emplacements and sculptures. I looked down the length of this gun barrel to where it would have fired on the invading force.

Farther on, the Çanakkale Memorial is the main Turkish memorial in this area. It is a sprawling park that includes sculptures, gathering areas, a museum and a symbolic cemetery with each headstone representing forty Ottoman soldiers killed in the region. The focal point of the memorial is the massive monument, beautiful in its simplicity. Thirty-five flag poles standing nearby fly Turkish flags most of the year. During commemoration days, however, they fly a flag for each country involved in the campaign, on both sides of the conflict.

A Newfoundlander's grave in the Lancashire Landing Cemetery, in the Helles region of Gallipoli. A tourmate kindly pointed this headstone out to me. I was the only Canadian on all three of my Gallipoli battlefield tours. (2015)

---

[33] Nicholson, G. W. L. (2007). *The fighting Newfoundlander*. Montréal, Québec: McGill-Queen's University Press, pp. 186-9.

Gun keeping watch over the Dardanelles Narrows, Gallipoli Battlefield, Turkey. Part of the memorial at the Kilitbahir gun batteries. (2015)

The Gallipoli Campaign

The 'cemetery' at the Turkish memorial. (2015)

The Turkish Memorial. (2015)

The Turkish people have a lot of national pride as shown in the architecture of their military memorial. They fly and display many more flags than we normally do in Canada. (2015)

A fellow visitor, reflecting at the foot of the Turkish memorial, looking out to the Dardanelles. (2015)

Facing page: Gallipoli Battlefield Helles Region. View of V beach from the Helles Memorial and Cemetery. This view shows the area the SS River Clyde ran aground. (2015)

33 The Gallipoli Campaign

Commonwealth headstones and the Stone of Remembrance at the V Beach Cemetery. The cemetery contains 696 burials (480 unidentified).[35] (2015)

Our next stop was the first landing beach – V Beach. Here, the invading forces beached the SS River Clyde, an important detail of the landing to get men closer to the beach and later provide support and shelter.[34] In this area was also the first of the Commonwealth War Graves Commission (CWGC) cemeteries I visited in this region of the world. At first I was struck by the differences between the other CWGC sites I have visited. In fact, until I saw the prominent Stone of Remembrance, I thought I was in a Turkish cemetery. Instead of the familiar headstones, graves were marked with smaller markers, set closer to the ground. It seems this was in deference to both local geology and customs of the Muslim country.

[34] Hart, P. (2011). *Gallipoli*. Oxford University Press, p. 71.
[35] Commonwealth War Graves Commission. (n.d.). *Cemetery*. Retrieved from https://www.cwgc.org/find-a-cemetery/cemetery/2000108/v-beach-cemetery/

Commonwealth War Graves Commission's V Beach Cemetery, Gallipoli Battlefield, Turkey. (2015)

The Commonwealth War Graves are much different in Gallipoli than in the other cemeteries I have visited. (2015)

The British Helles Memorial. (2015)

The Gallipoli Campaign

Etched into the wall surrounding the obelisk at the Helles Memorial are the names of 20,956 British servicemen who died in the region with no known graves, as well as those buried at sea nearby.[36] (2015)

Turkish memorial. (2015)

The Lancashire Landing Cemetery contains 1,254 burials (137 unidentified).[37] (2015)

---

[36] Commonwealth War Graves Commission. (n.d.). *Cemetery*. Retrieved from https://www.cwgc.org/find-a-cemetery/cemetery/76100/helles-memorial/
[37] Commonwealth War Graves Commission. (n.d.). *Cemetery*. Retrieved from https://www.cwgc.org/find-a-cemetery/cemetery/2000103/lancashire-landing-cemetery/

ANZAC Tour

I explored the ANZAC region – the region occupied primarily by the Australian and New Zealand forces – from two different vantage points, starting with another multi-stop bus tour full of information and opportunities for reflection.

North Beach memorial, location of the main landing beach for ANZAC forces at Gallipoli. (2015)

39　　The Gallipoli Campaign

A view of ANZAC Cove. (2015)

The Ari Burnu Cemetery overlooks the beach of the same name. It contains 253 burials (42 unidentified).[38] (2015)

An Australian woman looking out to sea, just outside Ari Burnu Cemetery. Whenever I look at this photo, I wonder what she was thinking about. Did someone in her family land on this beach one hundred years before? Did he return? Or, like me, was she simply reflecting on the conflict and paying her respects to all the men who fought here? (2015)

[38] Commonwealth War Graves Commission. (n.d.). *Cemetery*. Retrieved from https://www.cwgc.org/find-a-cemetery/cemetery/68701/ari-burnu-cemetery,-anzac/

This statue in the ANZAC sector depicts a Turkish soldier assisting a wounded ANZAC soldier. Although there seems to be no evidence of this event actually happening, I felt this air of respect throughout my visit. In 1924, Mustafa Kemel Atatürk (leader of the forces of the Ottoman Empire at Gallipoli, and father of modern-day Turkey) is quoted as saying, of the Allied men who lost their lives in Gallipoli: "There is no difference between the Johnnies and the Mehmets to us where they lie side by side... After having lost their lives on this land they have become our sons as well." (2015)

Turkish 57th Regiment Memorial and symbolic cemetery in the ANZAC sector. (2015)

The Gallipoli Campaign

Lone Pine Cemetery and the wall at North Beach are the main locations for annual ANZAC Day ceremonies on 25 April. (2015)

Lone Pine Cemetery, ANZAC sector. Burials in this cemetery number 1,167 (467 unidentified).[39] The memorial bears the names of 4,983 ANZAC forces with no known grave or buried at sea.[40] (2015)

---

[39] Commonwealth War Graves Commission. (n.d.). *Cemetery*. Retrieved from https://www.cwgc.org/find-a-cemetery/cemetery/66600/lone-pine-cemetery,-anzac/

[40] Commonwealth War Graves Commission. (n.d.). *Cemetery*. Retrieved from https://www.cwgc.org/find-a-cemetery/cemetery/78500/lone-pine-memorial/

The stalemate in the trenches of Gallipoli gave the Newfoundland Regiment a crash course in trench life and maintenance. In some areas of the peninsula, the trench lines were just a stone's throw apart – and a short throw at that. Even I probably could have lobbed a stone into the enemy's trench from my own at Johnson's Jolly.

Preserved Turkish trenches near Johnson's Jolly cemetery. (2015)

45 The Gallipoli Campaign

Turkish memorial at Chunuk Bair. (2015)

Chunuk Bair ANZAC cemetery. The cemetery contains 632 burials (622 unidentified).[41] The memorial bears the names of 852 with no known grave.[42] Perhaps many of them are buried, unidentified, in the cemetery. (2015)

[41] Commonwealth War Graves Commission. (n.d.). *Cemetery*. Retrieved from https://www.cwgc.org/find-a-cemetery/cemetery/66605/chunuk-bair-cemetery,-anzac/
[42] Commonwealth War Graves Commission. (n.d.). *Cemetery*. Retrieved from https://www.cwgc.org/find-a-cemetery/cemetery/76000/chunuk-bair-(new-zealand)-memorial/

My last day in Gallipoli was rainy. I spent the morning exploring and taking photos around the town of Ecebat, while dodging downpours. After lunch, I boarded a boat for a tour of the ANZAC area. In theory, the tour included snorkelling at a landing shipwreck. The rain meant the water was too choppy, so we simply lingered off North Beach and chatted about the landings while drinking tea.

The Nek Cemetery contains 326 burials (316 unidentified).[43] (2015)

Remains of an ANZAC trench. (2015)

---

[43] Commonwealth War Graves Commission. (n.d.). *Cemetery*. Retrieved from https://www.cwgc.org/find-a-cemetery/cemetery/66602/the-nek-cemetery,-anzac/

The Gallipoli Campaign

Of all the landing beaches I have visited, I had never seen one from this angle – the beach as the approaching soldiers would have seen it; the small strip of land they would need to storm and the massive wall of rock and dirt they would have to scale to meet their objective.

I tried to imagine being in one of the landing craft here or off Dieppe, or Normandy, or any number of other beaches - senses perhaps assaulted by the sights and sounds and smells of the landing as the time would come to jump into the water and storm the beach, even though the element of surprise was gone; friends and brothers-in-arms falling all around even before feet touch dry land...

I am certain my imagination failed me.

Landing at North Beach. The troops' objectives were the tops of the cliffs. (2015)

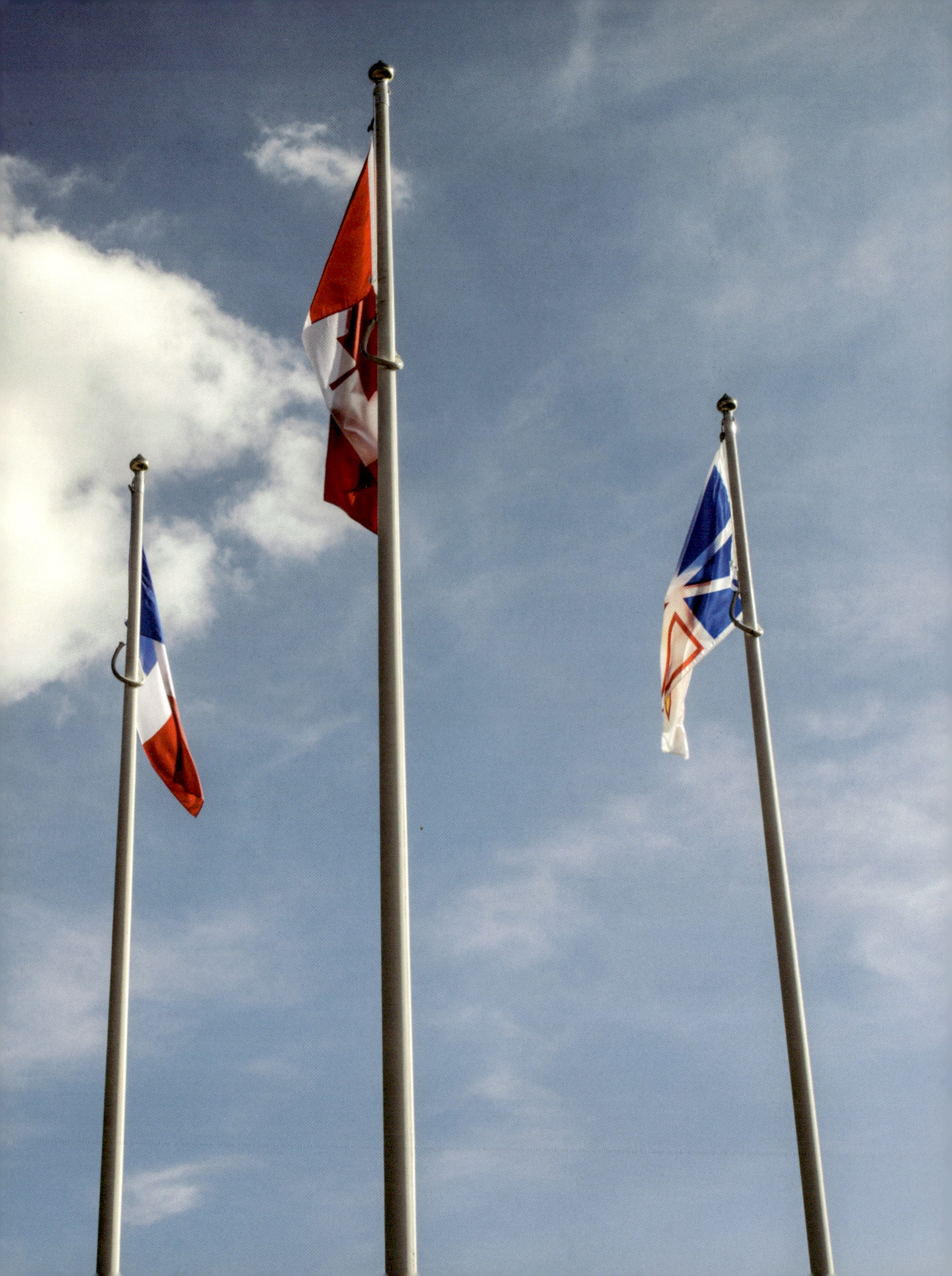

The Newfoundlanders at Beaumont-Hamel
The Somme, France | 1 July 1916

Of all the places I've travelled to around the world, there are still a lot of places right here in Canada that I want to visit but still haven't made it to yet. Newfoundland is pretty high on my list.

Canada Day is 1 July and in 2017 we celebrated our 150th birthday. Something I did not know until last year is that, in Newfoundland, it is also Memorial Day. On 1 July 1916, about 780 men of the Newfoundland Regiment climbed out of their trenches near Beaumont-Hamel, France and charged their objective on the opening day of the Battle of the Somme.

After the Gallipoli campaign, the Newfoundland Regiment left the Mediterranean in the middle of March and arrived back in the trenches on 22 April, this time in France.[44] Nightly reconnaissance runs, failed raids and five days of intense shelling preceded the opening day of the battle.[45] It was mostly for naught. They lost the element of surprise and the shelling failed to destroy the German guns or barbed wire, leaving only small openings through which to advance.[46] The Regiment went over in the third wave of attackers, with the wounded, dead and dying who had just gone before them lying throughout No Man's Land. Britain's Essex Regiment were meant to protect the Newfoundlanders' flank but their way was clogged with bodies and they could not advance. Following orders, the Newfoundland Regiment went without them.[47] They were the sole targets silhouetted on the horizon, weighed down with supplies, with the Germans waiting for them on three sides[48]. Slaughter was the only possible outcome. Silver triangles, meant to assist air reconnaissance and tracking, were literal targets on the backs of the wounded returning to their own lines.

Facing page: Flags of France, Canada and Newfoundland and Labrador fly at the entrance to the Beaumont-Hamel National Historic Site of Canada, in France. (2017)

[44] Nicholson, G. W. (2007). *The fighting Newfoundlander.* Montréal, Québec: McGill-Queen's University Press, p. 241.
[45] Ibid, p. 253.
[46] Ibid, pp. 265-6.
[47] Gilbert, M. (2007). *The battle of the Somme: The heroism and horror of war.* Toronto: McClelland & Stewart, p 116.
[48] Gogos, F. (2015). *The Royal Newfoundland Regiment in the Great War: A guide to the battlefields and memorials of France, Belgium, and Gallipoli.* St. John's : Flanker Press Limited, p. 116.

Only sixty-eight escaped serious injuries with 324 men killed or missing[49], including fourteen sets of brothers[50].

On this opening day of the Battle of the Somme, the Allies suffered 57,470 total casualties (including 24,000 Canadians) and 19,240 dead.[51] The battle continued to rage until November with Allied casualties numbering over 650,000. About 200,000 lives were lost on both sides of the conflict. The reward? The Allies managed to move the front line forward ten kilometres.[52]

The region is home to the Thiepval Memorial. Bearing the names of 72,337 who died in the area but have and no known graves, it is the largest Commonwealth memorial.[53]

Since 1917, the day has been designated as Memorial Day in Newfoundland, a Dominion of its own until 1949 when it became a province of Canada. The memorial park at Beaumont-Hamel, in France, is one of only two National Historic Sites of Canada outside of Canada (the other is Vimy Ridge).

Beaumont-Hamel National Historic Site of Canada

I have wanted to go to the Beaumont-Hamel memorial for quite a while. It is one of the handful of sites from my 2017 European tour that was new to me. It was, in fact, the reason I chose this tour out of the two choices I had narrowed the list of travel options down to.

Unlike other tours I've been on, our guide, Paola, encouraged everyone to take over the microphone on the bus and share our stories as we travelled from place to place. Some were stories passed down from people's families who had fought in either of the World Wars; others were of why we chose to come on this trip. Paola told us stories she had heard growing up about Italy in World War I (when

---

[49] Copp, T. (n.d.). *Newfoundland raises a battalion*. Legion Canada's Military History Magazine - The Somme, pp. 26-27.
[50] Veterans Affairs Canada. (2017). *The Newfoundland Regiment and the Battle of Beaumont-Hamel*. Retrieved from http://www.veterans.gc.ca/eng/remembrance/history/first-world-war/fact_sheets/beaumont-hamel
[51] Copp, T. (n.d.). *Newfoundland raises a battalion*. Legion Canada's Military History Magazine - The Somme, pp. 24-27.
[52] Veterans Affairs Canada. (2017). *The Newfoundland Regiment and the Battle of Beaumont-Hamel*. Retrieved from http://www.veterans.gc.ca/eng/remembrance/history/first-world-war/fact_sheets/beaumont-hamel
[53] Commonwealth War Graves Commission. (n.d.). *Thiepval Memorial*. Retrieved from https://www.cwgc.org/find/find-cemeteries-and-memorials/80800/thiepval-memorial

they were our Allies) and World War II (when they were not) and stories that she had only unearthed while preparing for this trip.

I ended up getting called to the microphone.

It may have been retribution for my persistent questions about this part of the itinerary. Our schedule said 'Beaumont-Hamel'. Every day, she told us what we would see in the following days, but she never mentioned Beaumont-Hamel specifically. So I asked her to clarify that we were actually going there. "Yes," she assured me. After that, she included it in her daily notes, but only mentioned visiting cemeteries, not the Newfoundland Memorial – the famous bronze caribou. So again, I asked for clarification and she again assured me and asked why I was so interested. Had I lost someone there? I was the only person on our bus from east of Ontario and I work with several Newfoundlanders. I almost felt as if it were my duty to visit this place for them. After telling her this, she asked me to share that story with the group.

Newfoundlanders often use forget-me-nots when observing their Memorial Day, as we use poppies on Remembrance Day. This forget-me-not pin was left at the base of the Newfoundland Memorial at Beaumont-Hamel. (2017)

After all that, unfortunately, it was a short visit. I hope I'll be able to return one day. I chose to spend my time on a guided tour of the site to get as much information as possible and then walked through a small section of the trench and around the monument itself before it was time to return to the bus. I didn't have a chance to visit the cemeteries, the Danger Tree or walk the battlefield. I laid a poppy (I did not have a forget-me-not) at the base of the caribou and took some time to reflect on the battlefield.

As I stood at the bottom of the monument, looking out at the scene before me, I couldn't help but think how far removed it all seemed from the chaos of battle. It was a beautiful day with serene wisps of cloud in the sky. A slight breeze rustled the trees and kept me cool, but it was not the crisp wind I have experienced on some of the beaches; there were no ominous storm clouds and rain as in Flanders. To my left, the land was a simple, idyllic, rolling green field; the closest cemetery so far away that it was easily overlooked. Surrounded by flowers and trees native to Newfoundland, it seemed at that moment to be the most peaceful place on Earth and that nothing bad could have ever happened here.

Then I looked ahead of me – down at the remnants of the old trench system, the uneven land caused by intense artillery barrages – like someone scrunched up a piece of green wrapping paper and made only a half-hearted attempt to flatten it.

A mosaic (and larger detail at left) of Newfoundland in the visitor centre is a montage of photos of the men who fought here. (2017)

The Newfoundland Memorial takes the form of a large bronze caribou, crying out. (2017)

Remnants of the old trench system and shelling at Beaumont-Hamel. Visitors are required to remain on the path in the park. Undetonated ordinance remains buried in what was No Man's Land. (2017)

Preserved trenches at the foot of the caribou monument are as welcoming as a beach-side boardwalk. I can imagine children have a lot of fun chasing each other through the twisting path. One can easily forget what may still lie beneath the dirt and grass and wood. (2017)

The Newfoundlanders at Beaumont-Hamel

The idyllic French countryside just outside the Beaumont-Hamel National Historic Site. Over 100 years ago, this was the site of the Battle of the Somme. (2017)

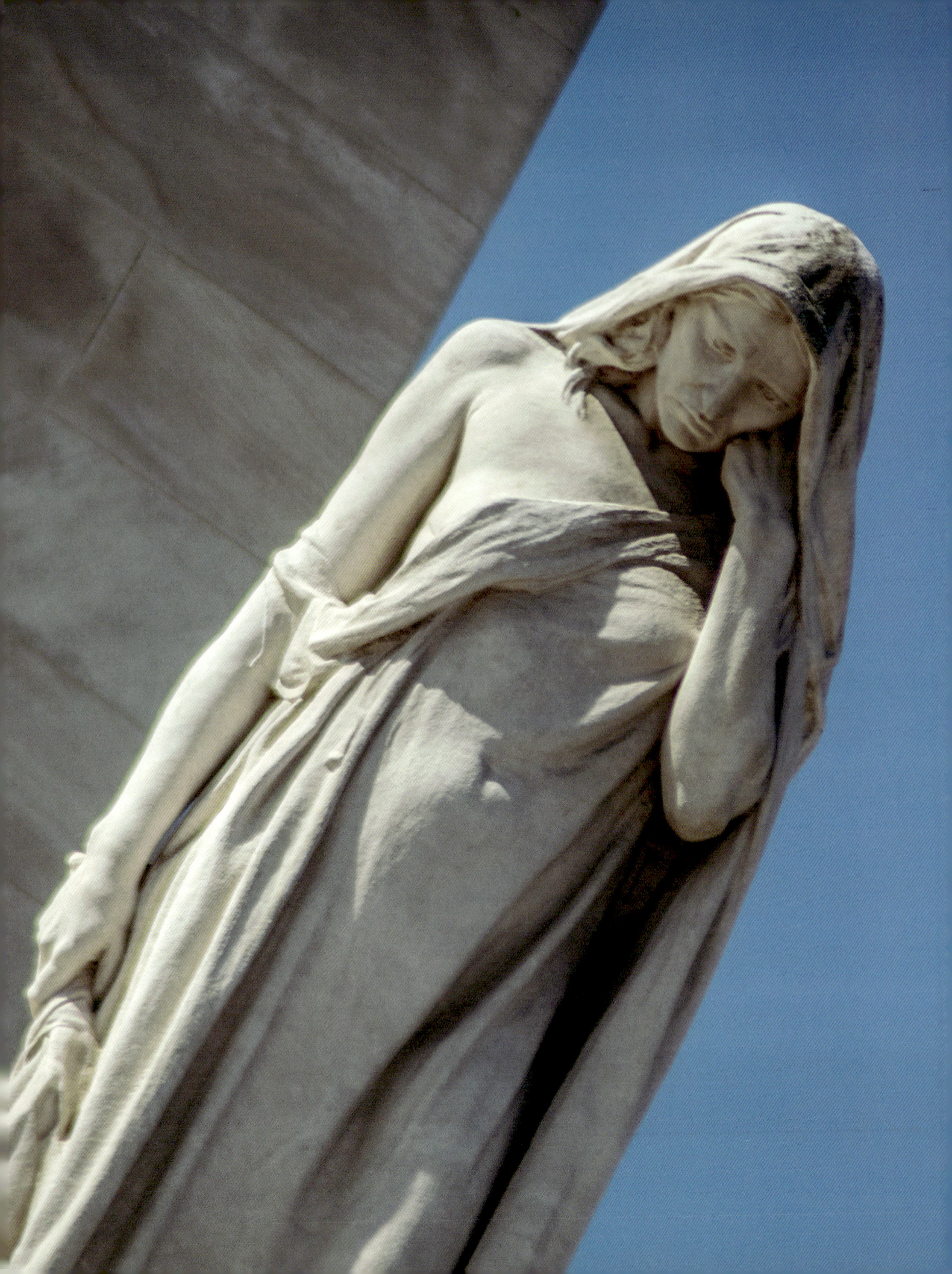

Canadians at Vimy Ridge Vimy, France | 9-12 April, 1917

Since the success of the battle in 1917, countless people have called Canada's achievement at Vimy Ridge the birth of our nation. It symbolized our unity and our military debut onto the global stage. There has been much debate over the years as to the validity of those statements, but 100 years later I too felt that sense of national pride on the ridge with 25,000 others, there to pay our respects to those that fought and died there on a snowy, muddy Easter Monday.

In 1998, I stood with my family on the steps of the memorial, the first major battlefield and monument that I visited. Designed by the late Canadian architect and sculptor Walter Allward, the twin pylons of the memorial towered above me. Almost twenty-seven metres high, they represented to me the strength that the Canadian Corps showed during the battle.

The Corps arrived on the ridge in the fall of 1916, relieving the British who in turn had relieved the French not long before. The German Army had taken the ridge two years prior, just a couple of months after the start of the war.[54] Later, the French made it to the top, but were unable to hold the position - suffering 150,000 casualties trying. That was 50,000 more men than the entire Canadian Corps that was tasked, with the assistance of a British division and support units, with the same objective in April 1917.[55]

The Battle of Vimy Ridge was meant to be a diversion, distracting the German Army from the 'real' battle near Arras. The Canadians had just seven hours to take the ridge and meet four specific objectives. Three of the four were met on time.

New to war as a nation, Canada approached the task with fresh eyes and new ideas. Bringing the four active Canadian divisions together for the first time was just the first step. Practicing decentralized

Facing page: *Canada Bereft*, also known as *Mother Canada*, is probably the most well known of the monument's twenty sculpted figures. The Vimy Ridge Memorial was unveiled on 26 July 1936 and on that day, another group of Canadians made the pilgrimage to France for the occasion. I met one of these men in a Paris café a few days before the Vimy 100 ceremony. He had been at the unveiling to represent his father who fought in the battle. This time, he brought his daughter and granddaughter. (2017)

[54] Humphreys, E. (2014). *Great Canadian battles*. London, United Kingdom: Arcturus, p. 304.
[55] Berton, P. (1986). *Vimy*. Toronto: McClelland and Stewart, p. 16.

Vimy Ridge rises in the distance, the white pillars of the Vimy Ridge Memorial standing proud. (2017)

command, division commanders had more freedom to lead their troops and trusted their men with more information about the battle. In addition to the countless trench raids to gather valuable intelligence, training was relentless. A replica of the ridge was created behind the line so troops could practice the assault. They also received cross-training to ensure smooth transitions and minimal delays when men were inevitably lost.[56]

Two weeks before the battle, the Canadians began 'softening up' the German trenches, dropping a million shells on the enemy.[57] They built more tunnels to conceal troop movement and perfected the creeping barrage – timing their advance with a curtain of artillery fire that preceded them. On the day of the battle, Royal Flying Corps pilot Billy Bishop noted the soldiers' practiced, almost leisurely pace behind the protective wall of shells as they approached the German front lines.[58]

Despite the preparations, the fourth objective – the high point of the ridge – proved more difficult than the others. The Canadians were short on men after suffering a gas attack a month prior and not adequately prepared. By the end of the day, the only fresh troops

[56] Humphreys, E. (2014). *Great Canadian battles*. London, United Kingdom: Arcturus, p. 307-8.
[57] Ibid, p. 309.
[58] Berton, P. (1986). *Vimy*. Toronto: McClelland and Stewart, p. 20.

available to the 4th Division were the men of the 85th Battalion – the Nova Scotia Highlanders. A work battalion, they had never seen battle; their usual weapons were shovels, not guns. Nevertheless, they rose to the challenge and, after a delay of just a minute to await an artillery barrage that never came, they attacked, taking the hill in an hour.[59]

Only one final stronghold, called 'the Pimple', and mopping up remained for the Corps. The battle was over by 12 April. Canada suffered 10,602 casualties, including 3,598 dead. The Battle of Vimy Ridge was not just a turning point for Canada as a nation - it was the first major Allied victory of the war.[60]

The scars of that battle can still be seen. So much of the ridge, and elsewhere in France and the rest of Europe, remains ravaged by the violent years of World War I and Two. The landscape is scarred with depressions caused by countless shells and mines. It conceals all sorts of war material including the most sinister – unexploded mines, ammunition, gas canisters and even bodies.

It was those pock-marked fields that made the biggest impression on me, more than the massive monument itself, or the headstones and etched names that spoke of families forever changed. It was the fenced-off shell holes and warning signs and stories of sheep having a deadly graze and farmers who don't just have to worry about operating dangerous heavy machinery, but what that machinery might dig up.

In fact, in 1996 France still had two million acres of land cordoned off, with artillery and other ordinance still buried, toxic and unexploded, in the ground. In France, the *démineurs* – France's weapons disposal experts – have the dangerous job of finding, collecting and destroying hundred-year-old weapons.[61] This is a problem throughout Western Europe. Even in our town in Germany we would often hear of farmers discovering military objects in their fields each spring.

[59] Black, D., & Boileau, J. (2015). *Old enough to fight: Canada's boy soldiers in the First World War*, Toronto: James Lorimer & Company Ltd., pp. 219-20.
[60] Tennyson, B. D. (2017). *Nova Scotia at War, 1914-1919*. Toronto: Nimbus Publishing, Limited, p. 124
[61] Webster, D. (1998). *Aftermath: The remnants of war.* New York: Vintage Books, p. 12..

Shell craters around the Vimy Ridge Memorial. (1998)

Standing on Vimy Ridge and reflecting on all this made me realize that in some ways, the wars are still going on. For some men, bearing life-long mental and physical scars of war, and some families, it never ended. It made me think about how senseless the war really was and how easily it can happen again. With all those thoughts in mind, I vowed, on that day in 1998, to return to Vimy Ridge for the centenary. On 9 April 2017, I did, along with 25,000 others.

The ceremony featured speeches by various heads of state including Prime Minister Justin Trudeau, Prince Charles and President François Hollande. Dramatic readings, dances and music highlighted our English, First Nations and French cultures. The *Commitment to Remember*, by Canadian youth and the *Act of Remembrance*, by Canadian veterans, were recited in English, French, Inuktitut (youth) and Algonquin (veterans)[62]. Before the official start of the ceremony, as everyone filed onto the field around the monument, we heard the names of all 3,598 men who lost their lives during battle. The reading took over four hours.

I found Prince Charles' speech to be the most moving. Using first-hand accounts, he detailed the horrors of World War I and both

---

[62] C. Gaudet, Senior Program Advisor at Veterans Affairs Canada, personal communication, 12 February 2018.

The Vimy Ridge Memorial in 1998. The flag of the United Kingdom was also flying when I returned in 2017.

the sacrifices and accomplishments of the Canadian Corps. He reminded us that it "was, and remains, the single bloodiest day in Canadian military history"[63] and he observed that many of those characteristics that made the Canadians successful in the battle remain a part of us today.

Hearing those words, looking up at that monument, being surrounded by all those other 'pilgrims' – so many of them young people, perhaps away from home for the first time, just like many of the boys the same age who fought and died where we stood – I certainly felt a strong sense of national pride.

---

[63] HRH Prince Charles. (2017). *Remarks on the 100th anniversary of the Battle of Vimy Ridge* [speech]. Retrieved from personal recording.

Designed by a Canadian, Walter Allward, the towering pylons of the Vimy Ridge Memorial represent the sacrifices made by the French and Canadians on the ridge.[64] In this photograph, I wanted to emphasize the feeling of them towering over the view, the same feeling I had standing beneath them. (1998)

Preserved trenches at the Vimy Ridge National Historic Site. (1998)

[64] Veterans Affairs Canada. (n.d.). *Design and Construction*. Retrieved from http://www.veterans.gc.ca/eng/remembrance/memorials/overseas/first-world-war/france/vimy/design

Canadians at Vimy Ridge

Sculptures adorning the Vimy Ridge Memorial. (2017)

Dozens of RCMP, veterans and active-duty members of the Canadian Armed Forces took part in the ceremony on 9 April, 2017. I created this silhouette to focus on the iconic symbol of Canada's RCMP. It makes me think of all those who lost their lives in Canada's conflicts, as well as all the people who refuse to forget them. (2017)

The Vimy 100 ceremony included music, song and interpretive dance representing Canada's English, First Nations and French populations. (2017)

(2017)

A feature of the ceremony was a flyover by Vimy Flight of replica aircraft modeled after the planes that flew over the battlefield in 1917. (2017)

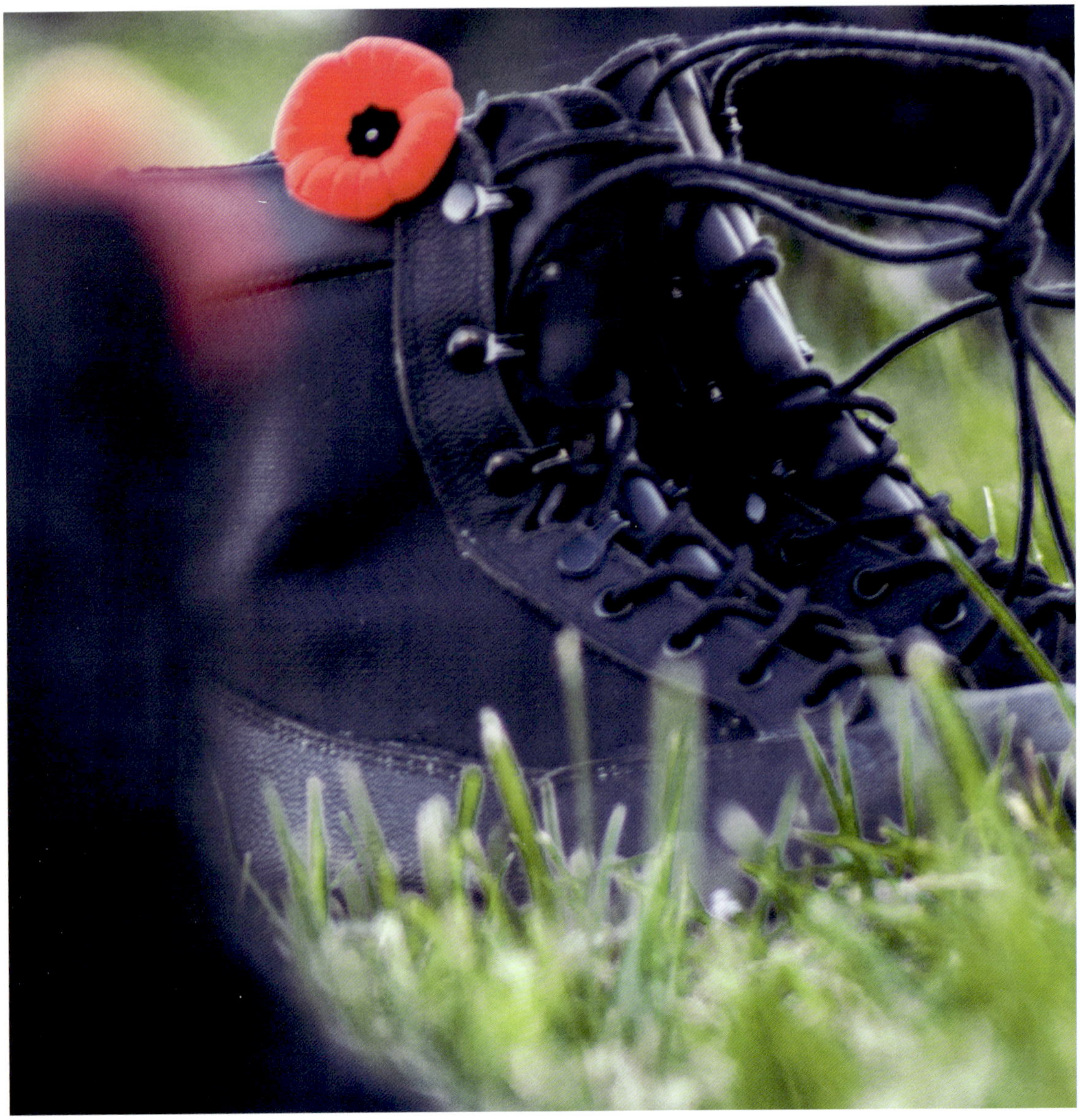

Canadians at Vimy Ridge

There are three Commonwealth cemeteries near the Vimy memorial, including a total of 1,037 burials (338 unidentified). The memorial itself bears the names of 11,242 Canadians who died in the region with no known graves.[65] (1998)

Above and facing page: Combat boots placed all over the memorial and surrounding ridge represented the men who fell during the battle. (2017)

[65] Commonwealth War Graves Commission. (n.d.). *Search Results*. Retrieved from https://www.cwgc.org/search-results?term=vimy&fullname=vimy&name=vimy&tab=cemeteries

After boarding the shuttle to return to our regular bus, we drove through the village of Vimy with so many of the houses flying Canadian flags. It was actually one of the most poignant moments of the day – to know that the community today still wished to share their respect and gratitude to the Canadians who lost their lives on the ridge near their home, so long ago. (2017)

Map of the Canadian National Vimy Memorial

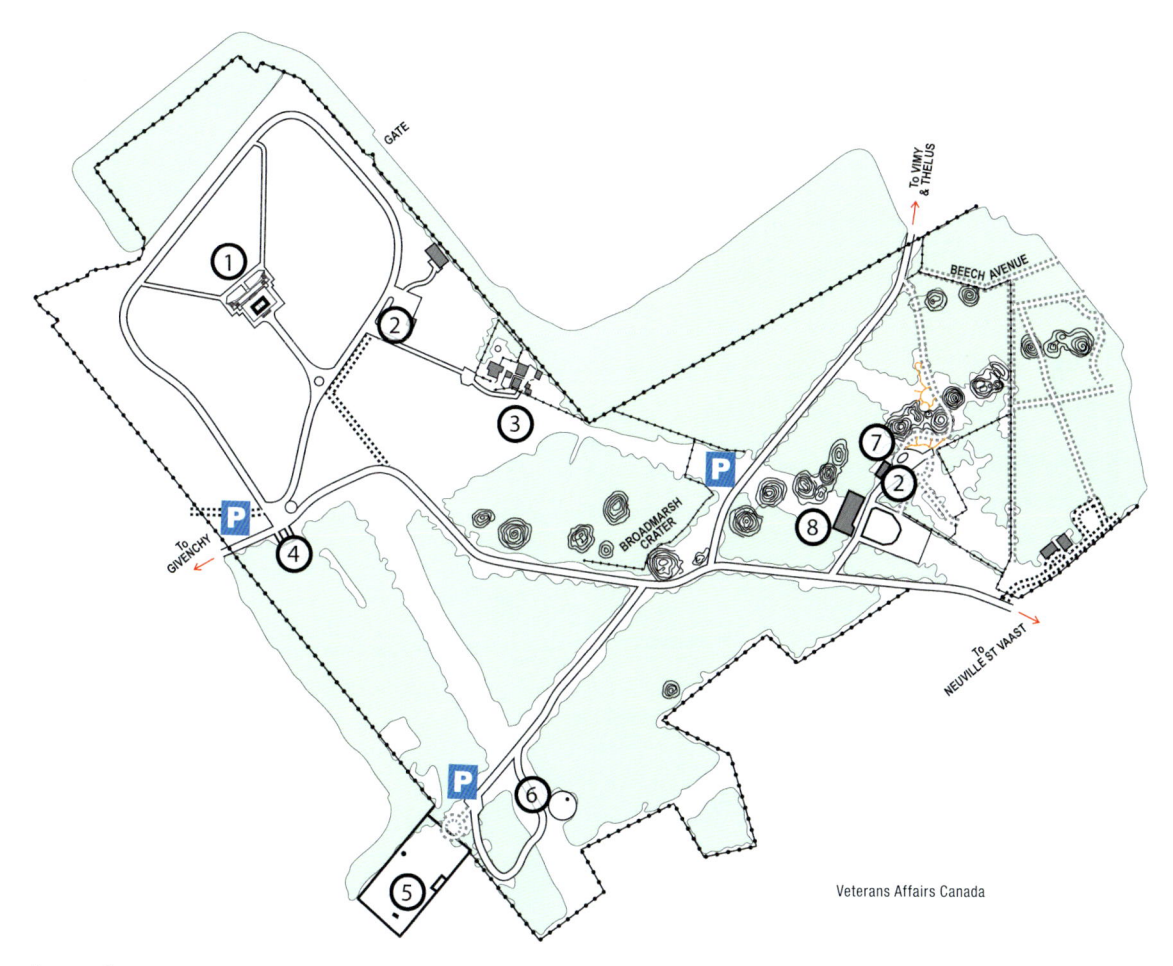

Legend

1. Canada National Vimy Memorial
2. Public Washrooms
3. Administrative Office
4. Moroccan Division Memorial
5. Canadian Cemetery #2
6. Givenchy Road Canadian Cemetery
8. Visitor Centre
   Parking

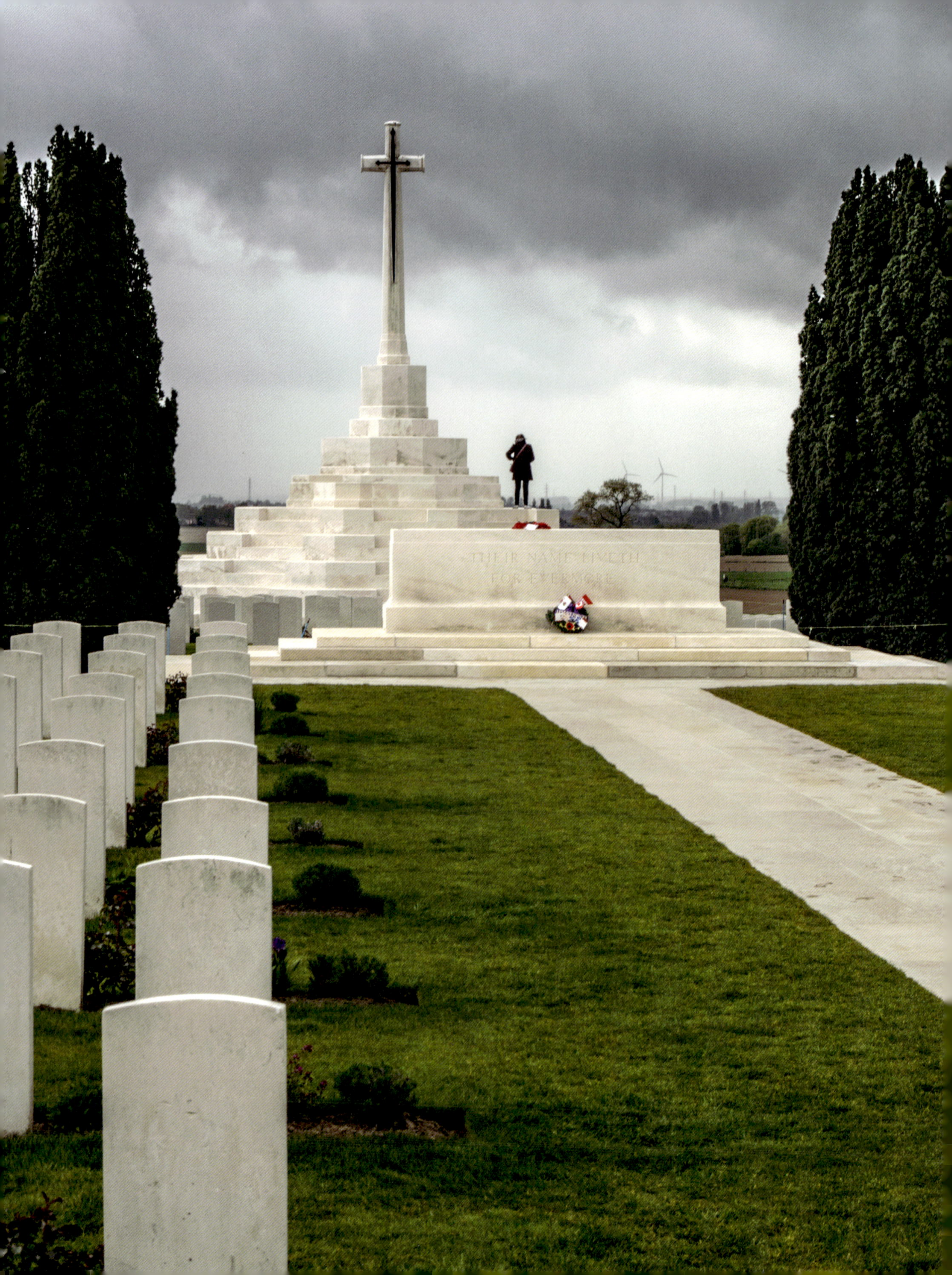
THEIR NAME LIVETH
FOR EVERMORE

Fields in Flanders   Flanders, Belgium | 1914 – 1918

As I write this essay, I am sitting in a local pub, watching the Gold Medal game of the 2018 International Ice Hockey Federation World Junior Championship. Young nineteen- and twenty-year-old Canadian and Swedish men are battling each other on a sheet of ice for a piece of gold around their neck and the pride of their nations. We think them so young, with their entire careers ahead of them. It makes me wonder about World War I and all those teenagers, and even younger, who lied about their age to fight – with rifles and boots instead of skates and sticks. They also did it for their country, the desire to serve, to prove themselves, to make their country and their families and friends proud of them.

At nineteen and twenty, these hockey players would almost be called 'seasoned' in those trenches, already older than the minimum military recruitment age of eighteen.[66] Despite the age requirement, approximately twenty thousand underage boys made it to Europe.[67] Some of them had parental permission but often they lied about their age and some recruiters turned a blind eye. Rifleman Valentine Strudwick, of Surrey, England, is buried at Essex Farm Cemetery in the Flanders region of Belgium. He was just fifteen years old.[68] Walking up and down the rows of headstones in cemeteries throughout Europe, I saw so many teenagers laid to rest.

Like their older brothers-in-arms, they hadn't expected to be gone so long; they didn't expect the horrors they ended up experiencing.

For many Canadians, when we think of the 'horrors' of World War I, we think of the battlefields of Flanders, near Ypres in Belgium. Ypres is the main town in the region and the hub for anyone visiting the area's battlefields. It might be the only battlefield of the

Facing page: Headstones and the Cross of Sacrifice at Tyne Cot Cemetery. (2017)

---

[66] Cook, T. cited in Black, D., & Boileau, J. (2015). *Old enough to fight: Canada's boy soldiers in the First World War*, Toronto: James Lorimer & Company Ltd., p.58.
[67] Ibid.
[68] Commonwealth War Graves Commission. (n.d.). *Casualty*. Retrieved from https://www.cwgc.org/find-war-dead/casualty/159930/strudwick,-valentine-joe/

war some can name. In elementary school, memorizing *In Flanders Fields* was almost as important as learning our national anthem. It is understandable. The area was hard fought all through the war, with three major Battles of Ypres.

The First Battle of Ypres

The First Battle of Ypres was fought 8 October to 20 November, 1914.[69] This month and a half long battle resulted in 238,000 casualties. Most of those casualties were German; they called it the *Massacre of the innocents at Ypres*[70]. Most of the British casualties were veterans of the Second Boer War. Even that early in the war, Ypres was the last town in Belgium held by the Allies[71] and they fought tooth and nail to keep it, even after it was reduced to rubble by the Germans during the second battle.

The Second Battle of Ypres

The Second Battle of Ypres (22 to 25 April, 1915)[72] was Canada's introduction to the war. The Canadians arrived on the line just before Germany started the battle with the first gas attack on the Western Front, dropping 152 tonnes of chlorine gas on the French section of the line.[73] Those who did not die fled, opening a hole in the line that the Germans exploited – though not as well as they could have. The 1st Canadian Division, sandwiched on the line between French and British forces, moved to repel the Germans and fill the gap.

Two days later, the Germans retaliated, this time against the Canadians at St. Julien with an intense bombardment and another round of gas. It was Canada's first significant combat experience and just the first time Canada would prove itself to the world during the war. In the first two days, one out of three men became casualties – two thousand dead and double that number wounded.[74]

On a busy intersection, once dubbed Vancouver Corner, near Ypres, the Canadian government erected *The Brooding Soldier*. Designed by

---

[69] Uttridge, S., & Catton, C. (2014). *The encyclopedia of warfare*. London: Amber Books, p. 771.
[70] Humphreys, E. (2014). *Great Canadian battles*. London, United Kingdom: Arcturus, pp. 288-9.
[71] Cook, T. (2015). Forged in Fire. In Betts, A. (Ed.), *In Flanders Fields: 100 years* Canada: Knopf, p. 36.
[72] Uttridge, S., & Catton, C. (2014). *The encyclopedia of warfare*. London: Amber Books, p. 771.
[73] Humphreys, E. (2014). *Great Canadian battles*. London, United Kingdom: Arcturus, p. 289.
[74] Ibid, p. 291.

Passchendaele Memorial Park. (2017)

Regina architect Frederick Chapman Clemasha, the pillar of stone rises above the small park with a soldier leaning on his upturned rifle, mourning his comrades who perished in the battle – specifically those who succumbed to the gas.

Total Allied casualties for the four day battle were almost seventy thousand. The Germans lost half that number, but were unable to break through the line. While the main battle ended on 25 April, the Germans did not end their offensive for another month. On 25 May, they turned their guns to the town of Ypres, reducing it to rubble.[75]

After this battle, the use of chemical weapons would continue, but lose their effectiveness in battle. Although both sides made improvements to their weapons, they also made improvements to protective gear. They would rarely be caught by surprise again.

[75] Humphreys, E. (2014). *Great Canadian battles*. London, United Kingdom: Arcturus, p. 293.

The Battle of Passchendaele

The Third Battle of Ypres is more commonly called the Battle of Passchendaele and was expected to be a quick, decisive battle. That is what the battle's planners assured but other leaders were not so sure. The latter proved to be correct.

It turned into a ninety-eight day battle, lasting from 31 July to 6 November 1917.[76] It was Canada's first major battle after the success of Vimy Ridge. The Allies gained one kilometre of land at a cost of over 700,000 casualties (260,000 German and 448,000 allied,

This Canadian monument is nestled in a peaceful enclosure outside the Belgian village of St. Julien. *The Brooding Soldier* stands in a pillar of stone "gas", leaning on his upturned rifle, mourning his fallen comrades. (2017)

---

[76] Uttridge, S., & Catton, C. (2014). *The encyclopedia of warfare.* London: Amber Books, p. 778.

Tyne Cot Cemetery is home to a sea of headstones. Too many of them etched only with "A Soldier of the Great War", "Known Unto God". (2017)

including 15,654 Canadians). That kilometre would be back in German hands within six months.[77]

Bombardments meant to destroy enemy defences did little more than destroy the area's drainage system. Coupled with almost constant rainfall during the battle, Flanders became the sea of mud we often identify with World War I.[78]

The battlefields around Ypres take up a small area, but are filled with so many cemeteries, monuments and museums it might take a week or more to properly experience everything with the respect that they deserve. I had a day each during my two visits. Four sites in particular stood out to me: The Menin Gate Memorial, Tyne Cot Cemetery and Memorial (the final resting place of many of the British who fell in the Battle of Passchendaele), Essex Farm Cemetery and Sanctuary Wood.

[77] Humphreys, E. (2014). *Great Canadian battles*. London, United Kingdom: Arcturus, p. 318.
[78] Ibid, p. 315.

Menin Gate

After the war, as the town of Ypres recovered, the Commonwealth War Graves Commission rebuilt the town's landmark Menin Gate as a war memorial – a large structure with halls filled with the names of 54,616 British Commonwealth troops who lost their lives in Flanders.[79]

It is *only* the total number of British dead in the region whose bodies were never recovered.

It *only* covers the first half of the war.

As I walked through the memorial, I ran my fingers across the smallest fraction of the names etched in the stone and reminded myself who they represented. Only then was I able to actually begin to visualize the sheer numbers involved in the conflict.

The architecture of the Menin Gate. (2017)

[79] Commonwealth War Graves Commission. (n.d.). *Ypres (Menin Gate) Memorial.* Retrieved from https://www.cwgc.org/find/find-cemeteries-and-memorials/91800/ypres-memorial

The Menin Gate, completed in 1927, became a hub for visitors and, every night since 1928 (except during World War II) at eight o'clock, wreaths have been laid and the Last Post performed. Each night the ceremony is different, depending on which visiting organizations, military groups and families participate.[80]

I attended the Last Post on Good Friday - 14 April 2017. The bugle call, as always, was haunting and mournful. In that venue, those feelings were magnified. Hundreds of us stood, silent, to pay our respects during the ceremony. We were surrounded by all of those names and a hundred or so wreaths left by visitors in the previous few days. A uniformed gentleman lowered the flag. The sounds of the military drill orders, the snapping of shiny boots on the cobblestones and that sombre bugle echoed under the arch. This was followed by silence, until the active-duty service members flanking the gate were ordered off.

Etched into the stone walls of the Menin Gate are the names of 54,616 British Commonwealth men who lost their lives in Flanders during the first half of the war and have no known grave. (2017)

[80] Commonwealth War Graves Commission. (n.d.). *Ypres (Menin Gate) Memorial*. Retrieved from https://www.cwgc.org/find/find-cemeteries-and-memorials/91800/ypres-memorial

78   Remembrance Road

Lowering the flag during the nightly Last Post ceremony in Ypres. (2017)

The beautiful architecture of the Menin Gate. (2017)

Tyne Cot Cemetery

The next logical stop on any visit to Flanders Fields is Tyne Cot Cemetery. It is Britain's largest military cemetery, containing 11,965 burials of World War I troops from across the Commonwealth. An astonishing 8,360 of those bodies are unidentified[81], their families never knowing for sure what happened to their loved ones.

Perhaps their names are included on the Tyne Cot Memorial that surrounds the cemetery. Continuing on from the Menin Gate Memorial, Tyne Cot bears the names of a further 34,991 soldiers known to have died in the region from August 1917 to the end of the war and whose bodies were never found.[82] The families of these men have only a name on a wall that they can touch. Perhaps some of them imagined that one of the thousands of anonymous graves held their brother or husband or son.

Headstones and the Cross of Sacrifice at Tyne Cot Cemetery. (2017)

Tyne Cot Cemetery and Memorial. The serene beauty of the Commonwealth War Graves Commissions' cemeteries belies the horrors of war that necessitated them. (2017)

---

[81] Commonwealth War Graves Commission. (n.d.). *Tyne Cot Cemetery*. Retrieved from https://www.cwgc.org/find/find-cemeteries-and-memorials/53300/tyne-cot-cemetery
[82] Commonwealth War Graves Commission. (n.d.). *Tyne Cot Memorial*. Retrieved from https://www.cwgc.org/find/find-cemeteries-and-memorials/85900/tyne-cot-memorial

Essex Farm

Canadian John McCrae wrote his famous poem on the battlefield in Flanders, at Essex Farm, in 1915. A doctor as well as a poet and veteran of the Second Boer War, he'd seen countless men come through his dressing station that had been carved into a hill. It was after one of his friends died that he was moved to write *In Flanders Fields*.

The wounded and dying in these battles did not have the sterile, well-supplied hospitals or clinics we expect to encounter when we are injured now, at home. Many of the soldiers killed in the war may have lived, had infection not taken over. What would it have been like to be there at that time, with the wounded being carried in, doctors working in horrendous conditions and without enough supplies, in the mud, with the drumbeat of shelling in the background?

As my aunt and I walked around the area in 2017, a tour bus pulled up and unloaded a group of Australian high school students. As

Essex Farm dressing station. (2017)

we did throughout most of our trip, we wore our red Vimy 100 jackets. In many places, they acted as beacons and Essex Farm was no different. One of the chaperones approached us with a few of her students. Our conversation started something like this:

"Are you Canadian?"

"Yes," we answered.

"John McCrae was Canadian, but we don't really know what we're looking at. Can you help us?"

I felt a flash of panic at being put on the spot, like I had shown up to class unprepared and been given a pop quiz. After a moment, I recovered and relayed all the information I could remember about John McCrae, *In Flanders Fields* and the site where we stood. I urged them to go into the dressing station, not only to view the memorials left by visitors, but to stand there and imagine, just as I had, what it would have been like that long ago, in those horrific conditions.

An information panel about John McCrae's poem *In Flanders Fields*, written here in 1915. (2017)

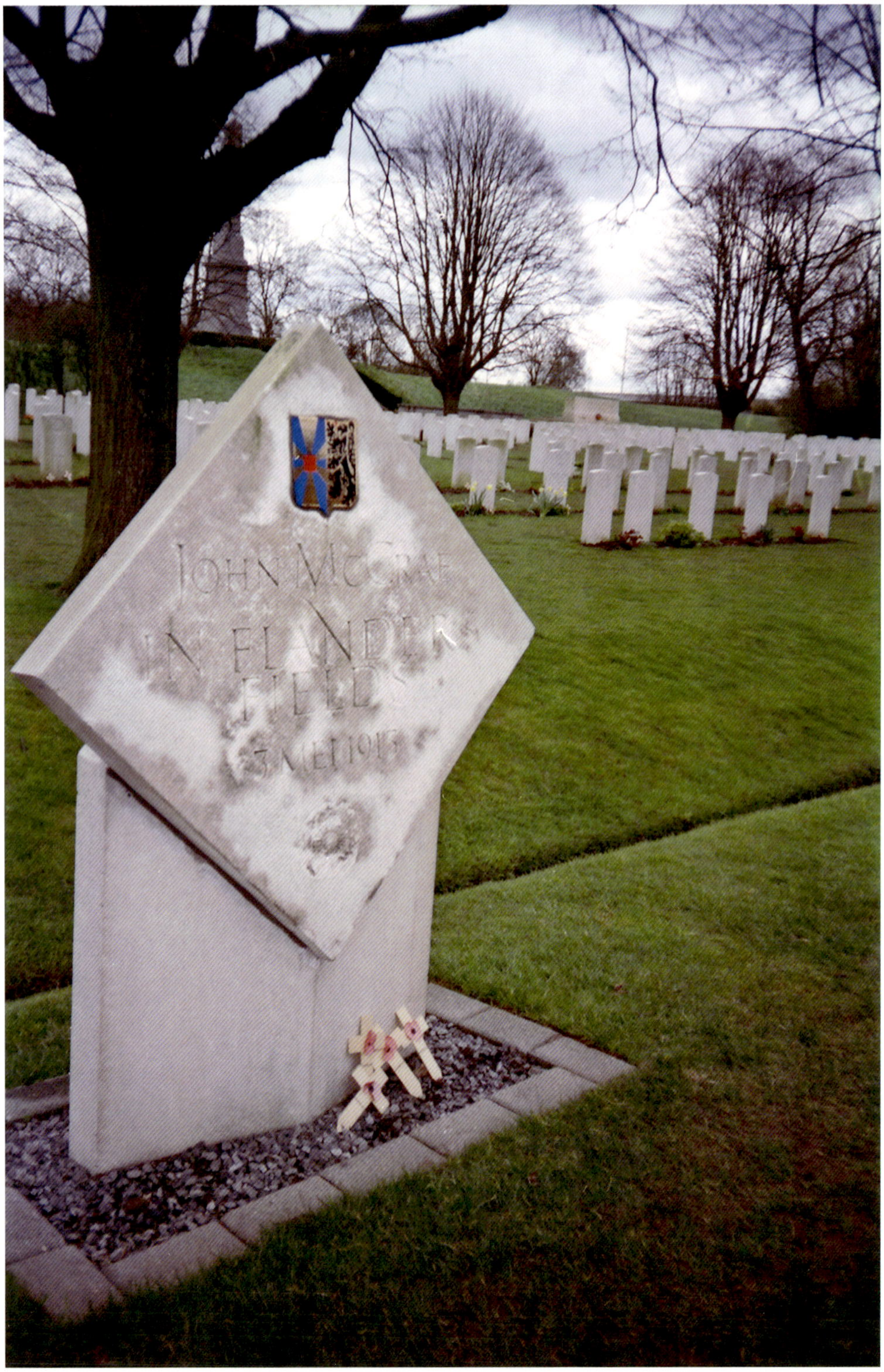
JOHN McCRAE

Fields in Flanders

Two of the many small memorials left in the Essex Farm dressing station. Looking at the dust and dirt left on this memento, I was reminded of the unsanitary conditions the doctors had to work under... and in which the wounded had to survive. (2017)

Facing page: John McCrae memorial at the Essex Farm Cemetery. Essex Farm Cemetery lies just across the narrow road from John McCrae's dressing station, bordering the Yser Canal. It holds 1,206 burials, 104 of which are unidentified.[83] (2001)

---

[83] Commonwealth War Graves Commission. (n.d.). *Essex Farm Cemetery*. Retrieved from https://www.cwgc.org/find/find-cemeteries-and-memorials/15800/essex-farm-cemetery

Sanctuary Wood

I first visited the Sanctuary Wood Museum, near Hill 62, on my 2001 battlefield tour, after visiting the D-Day landing beaches of France, as well as the other sites around Flanders. Over the course of that trip, it was not the miles of Normandy's landing beaches that affected me the most, nor the thousands of acres of manicured military cemeteries that paid tribute to the German, American, French and Commonwealth fallen, nor the tens of thousands of names etched into the walls of the Tyne Cot and Menin Gate Memorials.

Instead, it was this little café and museum in Belgium.

The approach to Sanctuary Wood Museum alone was enough to give me pause. I felt shivers as I drove down the misty, narrow, tree-lined lane called Canadalaan. Walking into the café felt so different from all the other places we visited throughout the week. There were no massive pieces of stone here; no modern visitor information centres. When we arrived, the only people around were a couple of men having a drink in the corner and another man who greeted us.

We were shown the little museum in a room off the café. It was filled with documents, battlefield finds and stereoscopic photo viewers that were like macabre view-masters. Even this felt different from those other, touristy museums. It felt old and settled – as if ghosts of the fallen stood next to their possessions and photographs and dared us to try and imagine a fraction of what they experienced.

Before looking around the museum, however, we ventured outside, around the back of the building. It was silent and overcast, the ground muddy from recent rains. A line of trenches, shored up with corrugated metal panels and filled with at least an inch of brown water, meandered through the clearing and back into the trees. Of all the trenches I have visited, these actually started to give me a sense of how the men would have lived and fought and died during the war.

The rains of Flanders are famous, and I thought that we could not have arrived on a more perfect day. Trench warfare was the horrible invention of what was then the modern war. Soldiers lived and worked and fought and died in the fortifications dug into the ground, surrounded by equipment and weapons, rats and the wounded and the dead. The scent of death and decay, illness and poor hygiene surrounded them; they suffered through shelling, bullets, gas attacks and the loss of their friends and brothers. In Flanders, especially during the Battle of Passchendaele, they did that through months of rain, flooding and mud everywhere.

We stayed in this 'Sanctuary' Wood for only an hour or so, in the mud, as the rain started again, and reflected on the sacrifices those men made all those years ago.

Fifteen years later, that image is still with me. It is impossible to imagine how much more the images of that mud must have been branded into the minds of the men who survived the War. Canada suffered eight thousand casualties here in 1916.[84] To divert

Stereoscopic photo viewers in the Sanctuary Wood museum. My interest in the history of photography originally drew me to the viewers. The visceral photographs depicting the horrors of World War I – half buried bodies in shell holes, desiccated horses blown into lifeless trees – in amongst scenes of the soldiers' everyday lives, made me sit down and look at every photo at each of the twenty or so stations. (2017)

---

[84] Tennyson, B. D. (2017). *Nova Scotia at War, 1914-1919*. Toronto: Nimbus Publishing, Limited, p. 88.

Trenches at Hill 62 / Mount Sorrel. These have been maintained, as historically accurate as possible, by the family that owns the property. Visitors can walk through the trenches and tunnels rain or shine. (2001)

Allied resources from their preparations at the Somme, the Germans launched an attack here on 2 June of that year, capturing the high ground. The Canadians fought back the following day. Initially unable to retake the hill, they did halt any further German advance and finally regained the hill on 13 June.[85]

In the end, neither side gained a thing; some men lost everything.

When I visited again in 2017, I thought not only of those men, so far removed from us today, but also of the men and women at war since that visit. They are not in muddy trenches in today's new, modern wars. Nevertheless, they still make sacrifices, physically and mentally. They still return home with memories that will stay with them forever and the rest of us can never imagine.

The trenches in 2017.

The battlefield of Flanders today. I wanted to show the peaceful landscape a hundred years later. The sky seemed to have different ideas. It rained during both of my visits to Flanders Fields. (2017)

Ypres – now an idyllic, scenic town one hundred years after World War I – and the surrounding landscape that was torn apart. (2017)

---

[85] Holt, T., & Holt, V. (2014). *Major & Mrs. Holt's battlefield guide to the Ypres Salient & Passchendaele.* Barnsley: Pen & Sword Military, pp. 100-101.

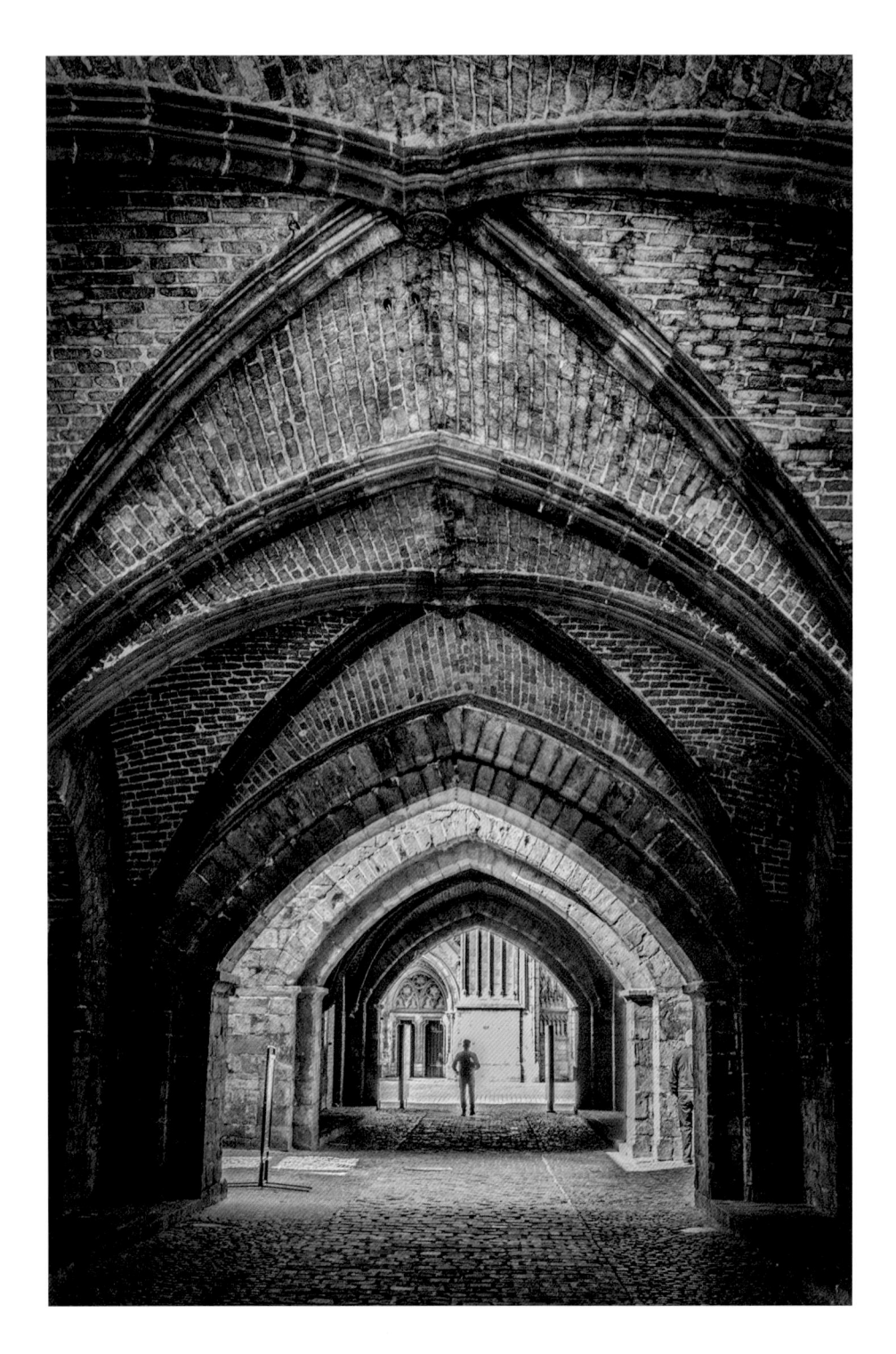

The reconstructed Cloth Hall – an important marketplace in pre-war Ypres. I loved the arches and the 'ghost' of the war I captured. (2017)

Fields in Flanders

The Cloth Market at night. (2017)

Part II

World War II European Theatre | 1939 – 1945

It seems to me as if World War II was a direct result of its predecessor – the war that was to end all wars; a war caused by one bullet and a collection of treaties and outdated ideas. Did the fallout of World War I cause World War II? Or did the political movements and civil unrest that contributed to the end of that war just continue to grow and reignite the fuse that had not been fully extinguished?

Almost nothing had really changed with the signing of the Treaty of Versailles. Trading land like hockey cards simply contributed to the continued ideas of *Empire* and the ruling of foreign lands. It added fuel to Communist ideas that began to take hold near the end of World War I.[86] After the Treaty of Versailles, many in Germany felt their punishment was too harsh – losing land and being forced to drastically cut back their military. There was one veteran of the war who was vocal and charismatic enough to bring all those people together.[87]

Adolf Hitler turned his experiences in the war, and his views on the Treaty and treatment of Germany, into fuel for his cause. He wanted to restore Germany to its former greatness. As this movement grew, it formalized into the National Socialist German Workers Party and they met en masse for the first time at Munich's famous Hofbrauhaus beer hall.[88]

He came to power in 1933 and was rearming the country within two years, rolling back limitations made on Germany by the Treaty. The following year, Germany teased the Allies by mobilizing its renewed military into the demilitarized Rhineland, on the border of Belgium, France and Holland and inching closer to the front lines of World War I. In 1938, Germany annexed Austria and then seized parts of Czechoslovakia.

Facing page: Dieppe Canadian War Cemetery, France contains 957 burials (187 unidentified).[89] (2017)

[86] McKay, J. P., Buckler, J., & Hill, B. D. (2001). *A history of Western society*. Boston: Houghton Mifflin, p. 917.
[87] Ibid, p. 971.
[88] Veranov, M. (2010). *The Third Reich at war*. London: Magpie Books, p.37.
[89] Commonwealth War Graves Commission. (n.d.). *Cemetery*. Retrieved from https://www.cwgc.org/find-a-cemetery/cemetery/2031200/dieppe-canadian-war-cemetery,-hautot-sur-mer/

Painted ceiling of the Hofbrauhaus, Munich, Germany. We were told the painted Bavarian flags hide decades-old swastikas. (2000)

The Allied Powers of World War I did nothing through all these manoeuvres – the memory of The Great War perhaps still fresh in their minds. Their neutrality ended when Germany took over the rest of Czechoslovakia the following year. Britain threatened war if Germany made the next logical move – into Poland. On 1 September 1939, Germany moved. On 3 September, Britain followed through on the threat, with France as its ally.[90]

By the spring of 1940, it almost seemed as if the British were beaten. The Germans had pushed through to the English Channel and surrounded the British on the beach of Dunkirk, France. By heroism or miracle, Britain was able to finally withdraw, but without its equipment. By the middle of that year, Germany occupied or was allied with almost all of continental Europe.[91]

Canada had mobilized by this point and the West Nova Scotia Regiment, who trained at Aldershot, Nova Scotia before moving on to Aldershot, England, were the only fully equipped land forces available to defend the island nation against the looming German invasion. When the Battle of Britain began, however, it took place in the sky, with up to a thousand German planes a day attacking

---

[90] McKay, J. P., Buckler, J., & Hill, B. D. (2001). *A history of Western society*. Boston: Houghton Mifflin, p. 976.
[91] Ibid, p. 979.

the island. The West Novas were the first in the Canadian Army overseas to take a prisoner in World War II when a downed German pilot found himself surrounded.[92] My British family passed down stories of children sent from their homes in London to stay with families in the countryside where their parents hoped they would be safe.

Popular science fiction movies remind us not to get too cocky – the implication being that it often doesn't end well. Cockiness is the only explanation I can think of for what may have been Germany's biggest mistakes: In 1941, with Britain still unconquered, the nation declared war on the formerly neutral Soviet Union, creating another two-front war. They made their second mistake later that year, declaring war on the United States of America after the Japanese attack on Pearl Harbour.[93]

Although the United States technically remained neutral until Pearl Harbour, the country aided both Britain and the Soviet Union. When they entered the war, they not only supported their own military, but increased their support to their new allies.

A line of tank traps along the German/Belgium border near Monschau, Germany. (2001)

[92] Raddall, T. H. (2014). *West Novas: A history of the West Nova Scotia Regiment*. Halifax, Nova Scotia: Dalhousie University, pp. 41-4.
[93] McKay, J. P., Buckler, J., & Hill, B. D. (2001). *A history of Western society*. Boston: Houghton Mifflin, p. 981.

When America entered the war in Europe, the Allies made three agreements. First, they would concentrate on Europe before turning to Japan. Second, they agreed to focus on military objectives first, and politics or potential peace negotiations second, to ensure they worked together more effectively. Finally, when peace did come, it would be in the form of the unconditional surrender of both Germany and Japan, ensuring that Hitler could not try and divide the Allies.[94]

August 1942 saw the largely Canadian amphibious Dieppe Raid. Delayed by weather, it was a failure, but one that taught many valuable lessons for the invasion of Normandy two years later. Lessons learned at the cost of 900 Canadian lives (just 50 less than on Juno Beach, and Dieppe is a beach many Canadians have never heard of) and another 1,946 taken prisoner (more than the total losses suffered by the Canadian Army between D-Day and Victory in Europe).[95]

During my visit in 2017, I walked just down the street from this park, taking photos of the town, and I encountered an elderly couple walking in the direction of the beach. The gentleman stopped me, asking "Canadien?", and pointing at my red Vimy 100 jacket.

I smiled and said "Oui."

His face lit up and he smiled. This is about where my ability to speak French ended, but I managed to understand most of what he said as we continued to talk for a few minutes. He pointed down the street and told me where I would find the memorial park, then pointed towards the beach, and finally out of town, towards the Dieppe military cemetery. I nodded and thanked him, not having enough French to tell him that I had already visited these sites and to share my experiences or ask him questions.

Before we parted ways, he shook my hand and said "Merci."

The beach at Dunkirk, France. Had it been a nicer day, and not a blustery, early spring day, I could imagine the sand full of beach goers, just like any other around the world. It is difficult to imagine what it must have been like for those British soldiers trapped here, wondering if they would ever get back home across the channel. (2001)

---

[94] McKay, J. P., Buckler, J., & Hill, B. D. (2001). *A history of Western society*. Boston: Houghton Mifflin, p. 983.
[95] Barris, T. (2004). *Juno: Canadians at D-Day, June 6, 1944*. Toronto: Allen, p.5.

95   World War II

The landing beach for the Dieppe Raid in August 1942. (2017)

Canadian Memorial Park, Dieppe, France. (2001)

Remembrance Road

97 World War II

Dieppe Canadian War Cemetery. (2001)

Facing page: The architecture
of Dieppe, France. (2017)

Memorial to the Airborne, outside the Arnhem Oosterbeek War Cemetery. (2017)

Arnhem Oosterbeek War Cemetery. The final resting place of Flying Officer Otto Hjalmar Antoft, of Kentville, Nova Scotia and others in his aircraft crew. Note how close together the headstones are compared to others in this book. I have seen the same arrangement with tank crews. (2017)

World War II

This bridge in Arnhem, The Netherlands was one of the main objectives of Operation Market Garden - an attempt in late September 1944 to follow up after D-Day and take out four bridges over the Rhine river to push into Germany. As the title of Cornelius Ryan's book suggests, it was *A Bridge Too Far*. Despite the massive airborne assault, the Allies were unable to take the bridge and casualties for both sides over the five day battle totalled 11,500.[96] (2017)

One of the many landing fields around the town of Arnhem. Taken at the Airborne Memorial. (2017)

---

[96] Uttridge, S., & Catton, C. (2014). *The encyclopedia of warfare*. London: Amber Books, pp. 826-7.

Arnhem Oosterbeek War Cemetery, just outside the town. The photograph shows the Stone of Remembrance, with the Cross of Sacrifice in the background. The 1,770 burials include 244 unidentified, about 70 Polish graves and a handful of Dutch and CWGC employee burials.[97] An Airborne memorial is located just a short walk down the road from the cemetery. (2017)

The Allies had almost no major victories before D-Day on 6 June 1944 – the turning point of the war and the beginning of the end for the Germans. The next 100 days saw the Allies push through to the German Lines – advancing through France, liberating Holland, taking key bridges over the Rhine in Operation Market Garden and finally, through the Siegfried Line into Germany.

On the Eastern Front, the Soviets liberated the Auschwitz-Birkenau Concentration Camp in January 1945 and arrived in Berlin a few months later. Germany surrendered on 8 May 1945 – the day after Hitler's suicide.[98]

---

[97] Commonwealth War Graves Commission. (n.d.). *Cemetery*. Retrieved from https://www.cwgc.org/find-a-cemetery/cemetery/2063800/arnhem-oosterbeek-war-cemetery/
[98] McKay, J. P., Buckler, J., & Hill, B. D. (2001). *A history of Western society*. Boston: Houghton Mifflin, p. 987.

101   World War II

Flower left on the Stone of Remembrance at the Arnhem Oosterbeek War Cemetery. (2017)

Map of World War II sites visited.

LE GRAND BUNKER
MUSEE
LE MUR DE L'ATLANTIQUE

D-Day Normandy, France | 6 June 1944

If the battlefields of Flanders are the most remembered part of World War I, D-Day – the Battle of Normandy – must be the one battle of World War II that people remember, if nothing else.

On 6 June 1944, after a delay for weather that probably made many veterans of the failed Dieppe Raid a bit nervous, Allied army, naval and air forces assaulted the beaches of Normandy in an effort to break through the defences of Germany's Atlantic Wall and push through France towards Germany. Along with other support units, American forces landed on two beaches code-named *Utah* and *Omaha*, the British landed on *Gold* and *Sword* and, with a fraction the size of the larger armies, Canadian forces stormed *Juno*, nestled between the two British beaches.

The first troops on the ground on D-Day fell from the sky. The British 6th Airborne Division crash-landed their gliders into France, just east of Sword Beach and the town of Ouistreham in the early hours of 6 June 1944[99]. Their objective for this silent, surprise attack? To take two bridges on the right flank and to slow down German reinforcements, in defence of the troops landing on the beach from the sea a few hours later. They succeeded in the task before moving on to their next objectives.

The armada approaching Juno Beach included 107 Canadian vessels with Britain's famous *HMS Belfast* as its flagship.[100] That morning, fifteen thousand Canadians poured out of landing craft to storm the beach. German resistance here was second only to Omaha. By the end of the day, 960 had been killed or badly wounded (not many more than the lesser remembered Dieppe landing two years previous). Although no Allied force met their objective for the day, the Canadians (and the Royal Winnipeg Rifles specifically) advanced farther than any other force.[101]

Facing page: An excellent museum about the Normandy landings in Ouistreham, France, just off Sword Beach. I visited the museum in 2001 and highly recommend it to anyone visiting the region. (2001)

[99] Kemp, A. (n.d.). *Pegasus Bridge - The first British assault.* Caen: éditions Memorial, p. 4.
[100] Beevor, A. (2014). *D-day: The Battle for Normandy.* London: Penguin Books, p. 131.
[101] Barris, T. (2004). *Juno: Canadians at D-Day, June 6, 1944.* Toronto: Allen, p. xv.

I visited the beaches of Normandy on two fast-paced day trips - one each during my 2001 and 2017 battlefield tours. The region, like Flanders, is filled with points of interest. It seemed as if around every corner I saw a battlefield, memorial, cemetery, museum or a sign to one of these places. A week in the region might not be enough time to fully take in everything there was to see and learn.

When my family visited in 2001, we left early one morning from Caen and drove down the coast of Normandy visiting Pegasus

Remains of a German bunker – part of the Atlantic Wall defences - near the Point du Hoc memorial on Omaha Beach. (2001)

Shell craters and a German Bunker at Omaha Beach. (2001)

Bridge before moving on to the beaches, driving until my dad had to turn around to head back to the hotel, missing only Utah Beach. The day included our first visit to a German war cemetery. We saw our first American one as well, but we at least knew what they looked like after seeing plenty of shots of Arlington Cemetery on American television.

In Normandy, it was the beaches that impressed me the most. Just like with many of the battlefields of these two wars, as you drive by

The Pegasus Bridge memorial was the first stop on our tour of the beaches of Normandy. (2001)

Britain's Sword Beach. (2001)

Beny-sur-Mer Canadian War Cemetery, near Juno Beach, is the final resting place for 2,048 service members (19 unidentified).[102] (2017)

Entrance to La Cambe German Military Cemetery, Normandy, France. (2001)

some of the landing beaches today, you almost wouldn't know that anything but frolicking in the water, tanning and the building of sandcastles had happened here. Juno beach is a prime example.

During my visit in 2017, when we concentrated on Juno and Gold Beaches, it was a beautiful, sunny spring day. If I were a regular beach goer, I certainly would have been drawn to the sandy beach and water's edge. Taking a step off the boardwalk and onto the sand, I could see nothing of the Canadian and French flags fluttering in the wind, or the concrete memorials. It was simply a seaside paradise.

---

[102] Commonwealth War Graves Commission. (n.d.). *Cemetery*. Retrieved from https://www.cwgc.org/find-a-cemetery/cemetery/2004600/beny-sur-mer-canadian-war-cemetery,-reviers/

Juno Beach

We started our morning, just a couple of days before the Vimy 100 ceremony, with a visit to a lonely stretch of sand near the new Juno Beach Centre. As I wandered along the beach, I thought back to my trip to Gallipoli and my boat ride and approach to one of the ANZAC landing beaches. From the little I knew of the geology and geography of this spot, I tried to think about what the approach would have been like on 6 June 1944. I scooped up a handful of sand and let it run through my fingers. Seventy-five years ago, the sand would have been full of ammunition, pieces of canvas and metal and wood, bits of uniform and blood.

It was my favourite of the three spots on the beach we visited that morning because of that feeling of seclusion and the subtle reminders of the war. I was able to sit and think about where we were and why we were there. All too soon, it was time to get back on the bus and head to the Juno Beach Centre - a new, state-of-the-art museum and interpretive centre focusing on Canada's contribution to the landings (and the largest museum I have been to in the region). It was just a twinkle in an architect's eye in 2001.

Beach huts along Juno Beach, just a short walk from the main memorial. (2017)

108   Remembrance Road

Entrance to one section of Juno Beach near the Juno Beach Centre. Just off camera to the left is a memorial art installation to the men who fought on the beach, but otherwise it looks like an inviting path leading to a pristine, secluded beach. (2017)

On the other side of the ridge, however, you find little clues as to the history of the place, like this small cluster of memorial crosses left in the long grass along the edge of the beach. (2017)

Sculpture on the grounds of the Juno Beach Centre. (2017)

Several bunkers remain on the grounds of the Juno Beach Centre. (2017)

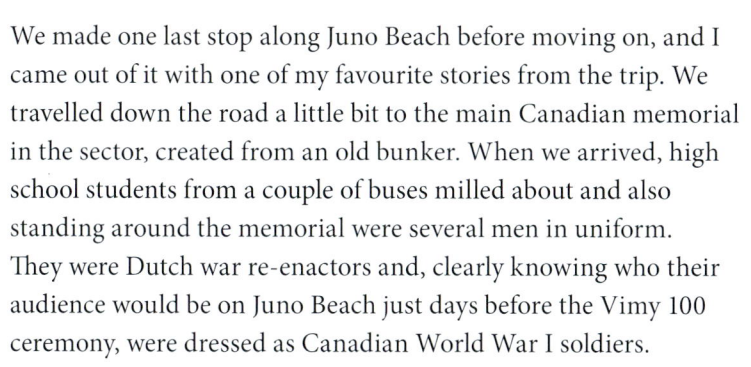

Path to the beach from the Juno Beach Centre. (2017)

We made one last stop along Juno Beach before moving on, and I came out of it with one of my favourite stories from the trip. We travelled down the road a little bit to the main Canadian memorial in the sector, created from an old bunker. When we arrived, high school students from a couple of buses milled about and also standing around the memorial were several men in uniform. They were Dutch war re-enactors and, clearly knowing who their audience would be on Juno Beach just days before the Vimy 100 ceremony, were dressed as Canadian World War I soldiers.

Entrance to the Juno Beach Centre. (2017)

We left them chatting to the students and continued to walk down the beach towards what is purported to be the first house liberated by the Canadians. After exploring for a few minutes, we headed back towards the memorial, where our bus was located. The timing couldn't have been better.

The re-enactors were lined up, standing at attention, in front of the memorial. As we approached, they began to sing *O Canada*.

Before they could get to the second line, one of the students' chaperones stopped them.

"Don't sing it if you don't know it!" He urged. I thought that was a bit rude – certainly these men wouldn't have started it if they didn't know it. He then continued, "We don't even know it!"

"Canada House" on Juno Beach, supposedly the first house liberated by Canadians in the sector. (2017)

I couldn't help but raise my eyebrow at that. Certainly not every single Canadian knows our anthem by heart – as appalling as that sounds – but it seemed in poor taste to admit that to these nice Dutch guys who seemed to think quite highly of our country. I can only hope that gentleman was a parent chaperone and not a teacher. But then the most amazing thing happened. Two busloads of students – I have no idea if they were all from the same school or not – started singing *O Canada* right there on Juno Beach. Canadians, in my opinion, have a quiet patriotism. That scene on Juno Beach was one of the most patriotic moments I have experienced. (And maybe, walking back to the bus with a smile, I felt a little smug towards that chaperone, thinking so little of his students.)

As I neared the end of a line of small Canadian flags left along the fence in front of "Canada House" by visitors, I looked down and noticed a can of corned beef. Also known as bully beef, it was a staple in World War I and II rations. A fitting tribute to leave on the beach to help sustain the ghosts of those who fell in battle. (2017)

Gold Beach

Our next stop was Britain's Gold Beach and the town of Arromanches. If Juno Beach was serene, with almost nothing to remind me about the war once I settled in to enjoy the sun, Gold Beach was the exact opposite. As we approached the town, we could see in the distance that this was not like other landing beaches today. Small black specs rose out of the water and when I first saw them, I wondered what they were. They grew as we approached, but it was not until I stood on the beach next to them that I realized how big they were.

They were the remnants of an artificial harbour used by the British to create a port where there was none and get men and equipment onto the beach. The Americans also employed the same method.[103] After the war, they remained on the beach and they cannot be missed. Any time the residents of Arromanches walk down the main street, or eat or drink at any number of the seaside restaurants or cafés, they can see them on the beach. They are not small memorials tucked in street corners, or tree-lined cemeteries just outside of town. I always wonder what they think about that – the constant, inescapable reminder of the war.

Or, seventy-five years later, are these remnants left rotting on the beach simply just something the younger generations played around as children and now do not give any more thought to? Perhaps they are just a collection of objects that tourists, like me, inquire about.

I should have taken the time to ask someone.

Remains of the artificial harbour in the waters off the town of Arromanches - Gold Beach. (2017)

Barbed wire and razor wire along the edge of a cliff above the beach. (2017)

[103] Desquesnes, R. (1989). *The landing beaches*. Editions Ouest-France, p. 15.

113   D-Day

Remains of the artificial harbour on the beach in Arromanches, France. (2001)

Just laying on the beach, these skeletons of the war have simply become part of the surroundings. As I took this photograph, children climbed on the structure beside me and on the other side, a couple more built a sandcastle. (2017)

I continued up the hill from the first look-off in Arromanches and came across another, with bunkers, a museum and this statue watching over the beach. (2017)

View of the beach from a look-off in the middle of the town. (2017)

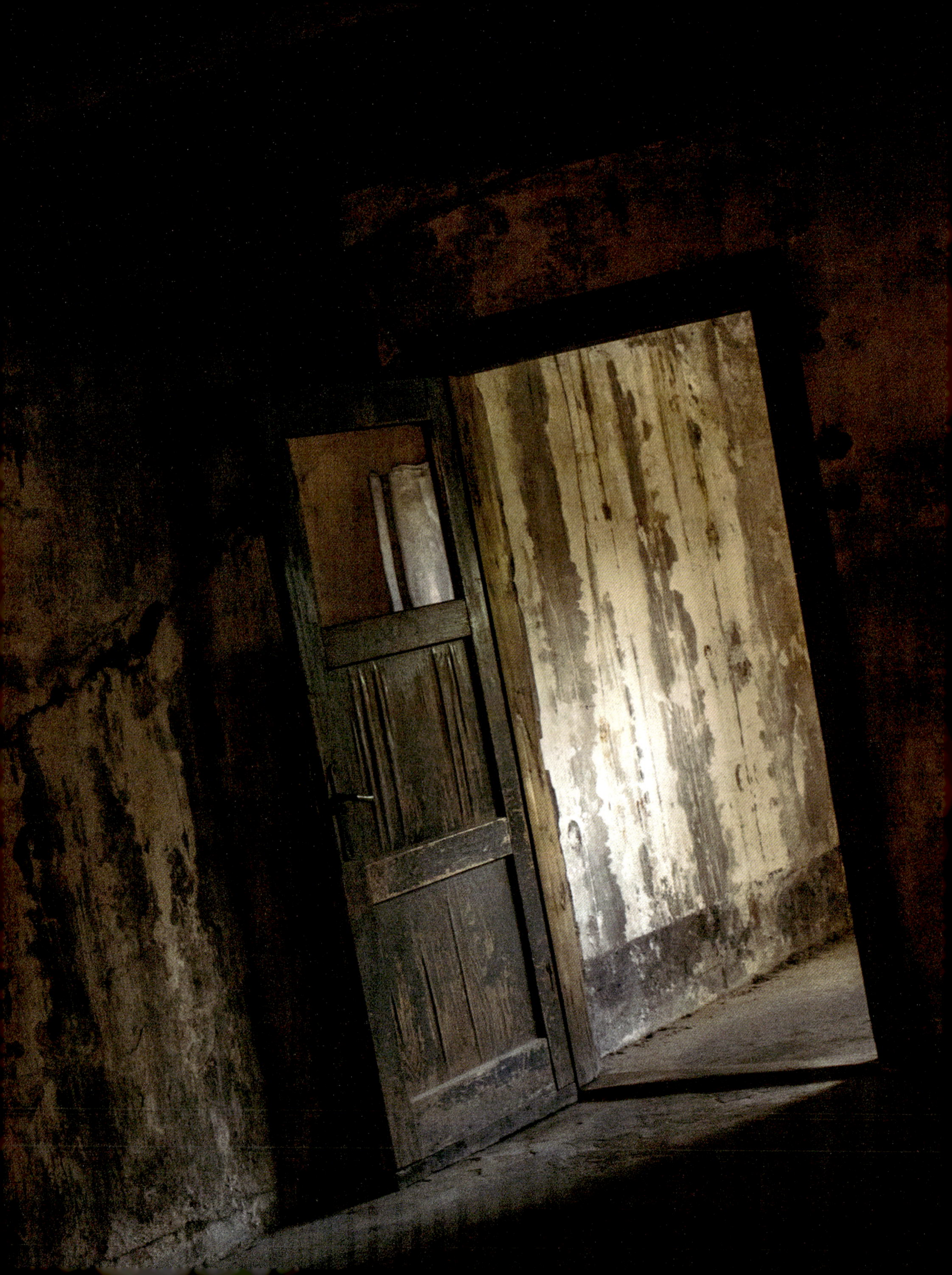

The Holocaust Concentration Camps and Transit Camps

Despite the harsh battles of World War II, it is the Holocaust that has understandably left the largest impression on the world. We do a disservice to the victims and their surviving families when we concentrate only on military casualties when we talk about the war. Of course there were civilian casualties outside of the Holocaust, and in other wars, but their stories are harder to uncover or follow.

It is difficult to give a precise number of victims, but six million seems to be the usual estimate - men, women and children. While the Jewish people were the main target for the Nazis, other groups were also persecuted in the Nazi concentration camps including gypsies, political prisoners and homosexuals. One of the most famous victims of the Holocaust may be Anne Frank, whose diary has been read by millions of people and whose secret attic hideaway I have been able to visit twice.

Victims would often be taken to smaller transit camps before being moved on to the larger concentration camps that we are more familiar with. Two of these camps were located in and around Mechelen, Belgium.

My first real introduction to the history of the Holocaust and the Nazi Concentration Camp came at Fort Breendonk, near Mechelen, Belgium, in 1999. My family took a day trip there and it was an eye-opening experience to see a museum like this, so different from everything else we had seen. The rooms were left almost as they were when the fort was abandoned near the end of the war, the walls bare and peeling and cold. The interrogation room sent shivers up my spine. Though it was mostly empty when we visited, it seemed to almost echo with the voices that were silenced at the camp decades before. Outside, firing posts and a gallows lined a small, grassy embankment.

Fort Breendonk may have been small, but the conditions were not much better than in its more famous cousins, especially as the war

Facing page: The door into the remining gas chamber at Auschwitz I. (2017)

118   Remembrance Road

Flowers lay at the base of firing posts, with Fort Breendonk in the background. (1999)

progressed. Soon, another transit camp opened down the road and Fort Breendonk shifted its focus to being a prison camp for political prisoners.

In 2017, as our tour drew to an end, we visited the Kazerne Dossin Memorial, Museum and Documentation Centre on Holocaust and Human Rights in the heart of Mechelen. The museum building is modeled after a guard tower and focuses not only on the Holocaust of World War II, but continued genocide and human rights violations. The ground floor is a temporary exhibition space and, by coincidence or design, during our visit they had an art exhibit installed that was focused on the "persecution of Native Americans".[104] The other floors lead us through a history of mass violence, as well as the history of the camp.

The original building of the camp stands across a small courtyard. It was the prisoners' barracks. The front wing of the building contains a small memorial museum highlighting some of the prisoners of the camp and a documentation centre. The rest of the building, however, has nothing to do with the museum. They are apartments. In fact, while we were there, some of the residents were

One of the buildings in Auschwitz I. (2017)

[104] Kazerne Dossin. (2016, August 11). *ROOD huid*. Retrieved from https://www.kazernedossin.eu/EN/Bezoek/Publieksprogramma/Tijdelijke-tentoonstelling/Overzicht/ROOD-huid

The Holocaust

Kazerne Dossin museum, Mechelen, Belgium. (2017)

in the courtyard chatting and children screeched and ran around, as children do.

I wondered what it was like to live in an apartment that, not all that long ago housed prisoners on their way to Auschwitz or other concentration camps.

They did look like quite nice apartments.

From transit camps like these, scattered throughout Europe, prisoners were transferred to concentration or extermination camps, also located throughout Europe, though concentrated in Germany and Poland. Many excellent books have been written on the subject, so I will not provide an extensive history here, but I do encourage you to read them. As signs throughout both the Kazerne Dossin and Auschwitz museums stated - we must remember and learn from the past. Nothing else will stop it from happening again.

The original prisoners' barracks of the Kazerne Dossin, now apartments and a small documentation centre. I took this photograph from the observation tower of the museum across the courtyard. (2017)

Dachau Concentration Camp was liberated by shocked American forces in April 1945.[105] Like similar sites, it soon became a memorial and museum. Those men may have known the Nazis were committing horrible crimes, but it wasn't until they entered the camp that day that they started to understand exactly what had happened there.

In the summer of 2000, we spent a couple of weeks on vacation in Bavaria. One day, we decided to go in to Munich. We spent the morning exploring the city before driving to the Dachau Concentration Camp Memorial Site.

I do not recall there being many buildings left at the site; most of the buildings' footprints were simply outlined on the ground. To be honest, I do not remember much about that afternoon at all. I do remember walking through the exhibits in the museum and trying to come to terms with the information on display; to try and let the visuals coalesce into something that made sense.

But nothing about it really made sense.

I think it was the sculpture in the courtyard outside the museum that made the most lasting impression on me. It screamed pain to me; looking at it was painful and still is.

Dachau gave me that feeling of 'pain' but it was not until I visited Auschwitz that those visuals started to finally make some kind of sense. Maybe it was because it was so much bigger than Dachau, or because I was older, or because I had done more research in the previous eighteen years.

My aunt and I visited the Auschwitz-Birkenau Memorial and Museum for an eight hour tour at the end of our 2017 battlefield trip. The camp was originally made up of several smaller facilities and the current museum consists of the original Auschwitz I and

Cremation oven at Dachau. (2000)

---

[105] Dann, S. (1998). *Dachau 29 April 1945: The Rainbow liberation memoirs.* Lubbock, TX: Texas Tech University Press, p. vii.

Auschwitz II-Birkenau camps. We had a guide for the entire tour and started the morning at Auschwitz I before taking a shuttle after lunch to Auschwitz II-Birkenau.

Auschwitz I is the main museum. It includes a couple of buildings with artefacts, a massive room-sized book listing the name of every victim of the Holocaust and where they were murdered, multimedia presentations telling survivor stories and other documentation, as well as several buildings kept in their original state and accessible only with the guide. Auschwitz II-Birkenau is a collection of buildings, ruins and memorials.

Sculpture at Dachau Concentration Camp, near Munich, Germany. (2000)

The famous sign proclaiming "work will make you free" at the entrance of many concentration camps, including Dachau and here at Auschwitz. (2017)

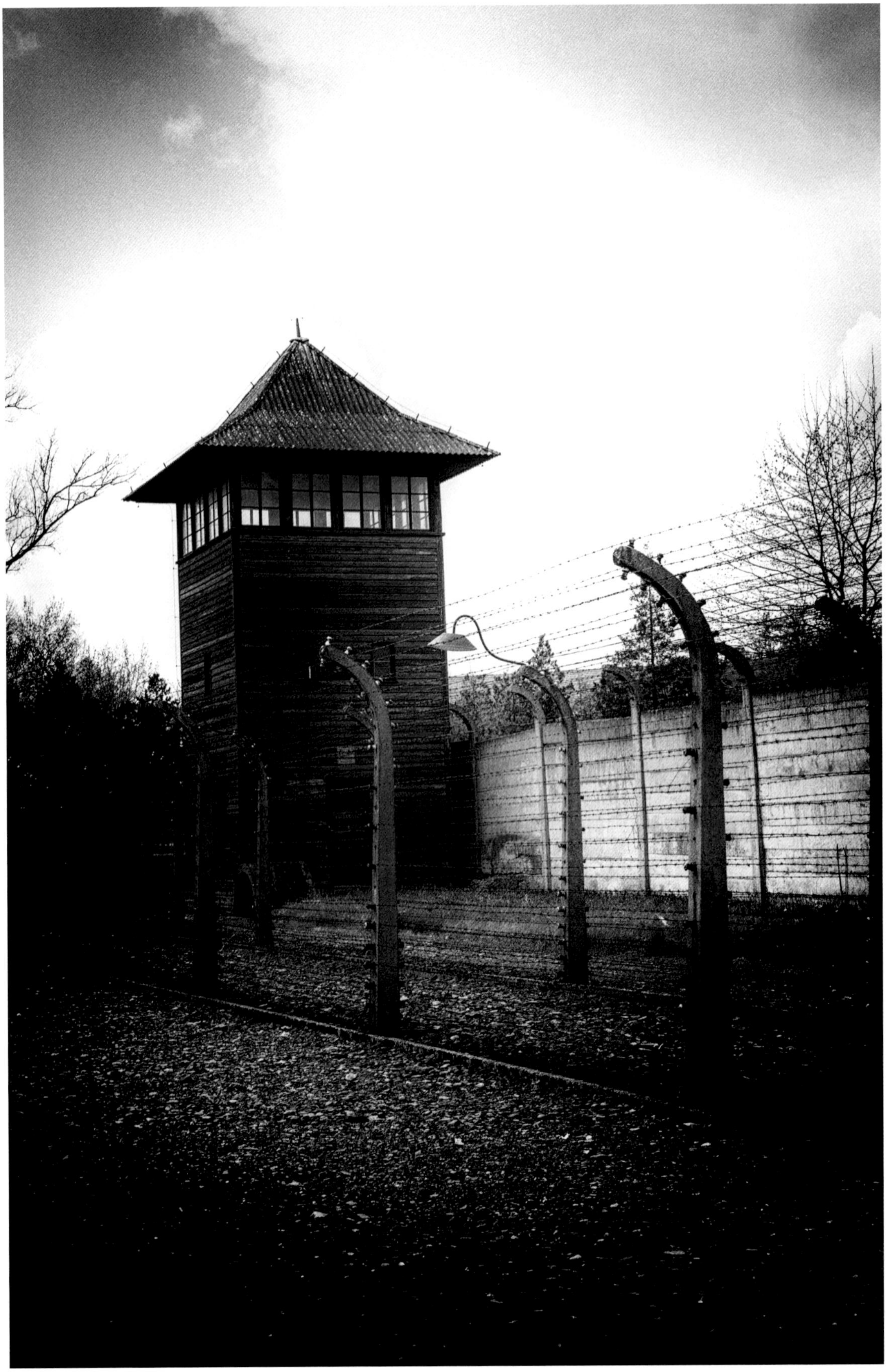

123　　The Holocaust

I chose to process these 'street scenes' of the Auschwitz Concentration Camp as black and white, foreboding, almost gritty images as a way to try and convey a feeling of fear and darkness. (2017)

One fact given to us by our guide that stood out to me referenced some warehouses. When victims were rounded up from their homes, they were told only that they were relocating, so they brought the things they thought they would need in their new lives - things like dishes and clothing. When they arrived off the train, all of their possessions were taken from them and stored in these warehouses.

The warehouses were called Kanada I and Kanada II because, he told us, Canada was thought to be a land of plenty and, as such, was a fitting name for a warehouse storing plenty of family possessions. The Nazis destroyed the warehouses and many of those possessions as the Russians neared the camp. The belongings that remained are on display in the museum as a way to help the visitor visualize the numbers and lives of the people who were murdered here.

The most striking collection was inside a darkened room. Behind the glass was a thick blanket of human hair. Before being locked, naked, inside the gas chambers, the victims were also shorn of their hair, which was then sold to various German companies. The companies made use of the hair for things such as weaving and stuffing.

We learned that the Germans destroyed most of those gas chambers before the camp was liberated, the rubble still lying as it fell when it was destroyed. The one that remains was the first gas chamber built, the only one built above ground. Those in charge of the gas chambers quickly learned that building them into the ground was a better idea. To start, it made it easier to drop the gas canisters through the ceiling.

It also muffled the screams.

There was one 'problem' with the gas chambers. They could kill up to 300 people at a time, but with only two ovens for each gas chamber, they could not dispose of the bodies as fast as they created them.

Auschwitz-Birkenau Memorial and Museum. (2017)

Belongings of a small portion of the victims of the Auschwitz Concentration Camp. (2017)

Small memorials left by visitors around the camp. (2017)

The nauseating feeling I had at Fort Breendonk only intensified here. Still, I noticed something else during those eight hours. Through all the darkness, there were flashes of colour - hints of peace and hope: A colourful chain of origami cranes. A candle. A sprig of flowers. A painted rock.........

Proof that people still remembered and would never forget.

The Holocaust

A gate leading into Auschwitz II-Birkenau. (2017)

129   The Holocaust

Auschwitz II-Birkenau from the observation tower at the main entrance. (2017)

Destroyed gas chamber. (2017)

A small section of the Book of Names – a record of all the victims of the Holocaust. The book is almost as large as the room it's housed in at the Auschwitz-Birkenau Memorial and Museum. (2017)

Crematorium at the Auschwitz-Birkenau Memorial and Museum. (2017)

A few of the remaining personal effects of the victims of the Auschwitz concentration camp. (2017)

PETERS	POP...
PETERS ...RITZ	PO... CHE W...
...HEINRICH	PRAC...
...HEINRICH	PRAHL W...
...RS HERMANN	PRANGE F...
...S HERMANN	PRANGE M.
...RS JAKOB	PRENZLIN...
...S JOHANN	PRESSLER FRI...
...JOHANNES	PREUS...
PETERS ...OTTO	PREUS...
PETERS R...	PP... RICHA...
PETERSDORF...	...OSS WILHE...
PETERSDOR...	...BBERNOW E...
PETERSEN F...	...BBERNOW K.
PETERSEN H...	...CHE HA...
PETERSEN ...O	...GE THEOD...
...JA...	PR... HAN...
...N JOHS.	PRIES... UGU...
...ERSEN JOHS.	PRIES...
...ERSEN JOHS.	PRIESEMU...
...N KARL	PRIETZ K...
...N MAX	PRINTZEN JO...
...RUDOLF	PRINZ
...N MAX	PRINZLE...
	PRITZKU...

Remembering the Dead Military Cemeteries of World Wars I and II

Landing beaches, manicured trenches, jagged fields – these all require some imagination to fully appreciate what happened seventy-five or a hundred years ago. Trees have returned, the weather is lovely and towns have been rebuilt or grown around them. Some people just are not equipped with that kind of imagination, especially if they have not done a lot of research into the wars.

One thing that requires no imagination is the military cemetery. Their sheer number is astonishing.

The Commonwealth War Graves Commission was created early in World War I to deal with the huge number of fallen. Death in World War I was vicious, indiscriminate and on a scale not seen in living memory.

By the end of that war, the Commission was responsible for the burials of almost half a million Commonwealth dead.[106] Total military dead and missing on both sides of the conflict reached almost ten million.[107] It may not have been the bloodiest war in history, but for Britain it was the worst war anyone could remember. Certainly the global scale of the four year war, as well as the conditions the soldiers dealt with, were unprecedented.

The Allies went into the war fighting as they had every other war they could remember. It took time to adapt to this new war. Machine guns replaced rifles and artillery barrages were so intense and sustained that munitions factories quickly depleted their supply and often struggled to keep up. But adapt they did. By the end of the war they perfected artillery targeting, learned the art of the artillery curtain and employed aircraft.

Twenty years later, they had to do it all over again.

Facing page: Inside the entrance to the Langemark cemetery (at one end of the mass grave) visitors will find wooden panels listing names of soldiers believed to be buried in the cemetery, but whose bodies could not be identified. (2017)

[106] Longworth, P. (2003). *The unending vigil: A history of the Commonwealth War Graves Commission.* Barnsley, S. Yorkshire: Leo Cooper, p.124.
[107] McKay, J. P., Buckler, J., & Hill, B. D. (2001). *A history of Western society.* Boston: Houghton Mifflin, p. 916.

The war killed indiscriminately. It cared not which social class a regular soldier or officer came from. By this time, the Allies were more interested in maintaining the individuality of the soldier than they previously had been, helped out, if not effected, by better identification techniques. This caused Britain to find a way to deal with the dead equally in a way, and on a scale, that they never needed to before. With an empire as vast as Britain's, the organizers also had to find a way to incorporate other faiths and cultural practices.

The task of compromise and negotiation was not an easy one, and it started almost immediately. The CWGC formed out of the Red Cross. Once the decision was made not to repatriate the bodies, it was the Commission's task to negotiate a gift of land for a cemetery – even while the host nations were still involved in the war and later, in rebuilding and burying their own dead. Then they needed to design and build the cemeteries and continue to maintain them in perpetuity. The Commission has entered its second century

Dieppe Canadian War Cemetery, France. This photo features several differences between gravestones. Brigadier Mary Climpson, of the Salvation Army in the United Kingdom was not only the sole woman whose grave I had seen, but one of the oldest service members I've noticed during my visits to the European military cemeteries. Private Abse, a Jewish teenager serving with Britain's Royal Army Medical Corps, is buried next to her. Both fell in this area two years before the Dieppe Raid. (2017)

of operation and their work restoring vandalized or destroyed cemeteries in current conflict zones, maintaining headstones and landscaping continues. They even still conduct new burials.

Some war material remains buried in the battlefields, but that is not everything that the earth could give back to us. While it is generally not the Commission's practice to search for bodies, new ones continue to be found or identifications are made.

The Commission also oversaw the placement of memorials, such as the Menin Gate in Ypres and the Theipval Memorial on the battlefield of The Somme, to try and help the host nations from being inundated by them. I am not sure how successful they were in that goal. As it is, the CWGC created 2,500 World War I and World War II cemeteries and memorials, choosing to bury soldiers more or less where they fought and died. They range in size from a handful of burials in Cemeteries like Plugge's Plateau Cemetery in Gallipoli[108] to Britain's largest military cemetery Tyne Cot in Belgium with 11,965 burials and 34,951 names on the memorial to the missing.[109]

The headstones are all uniform, with a few exceptions for local political, cultural or climate conditions (as in Gallipoli), and feature a cross, other religious emblem, or regimental badge. Many Canadian headstones feature a maple leaf. Their name, rank, date of death, age and a short inscription are carved into the stone. Some simply say "A soldier of the Great War... Known Unto God" – where a body was recovered, but no positive identification was possible. Whenever possible, everyone was given an individual burial.

In total, the Commission is now responsible for the maintenance of burials and memorials commemorating 1.7 Million World War I and World War II service members in 23,000 locations

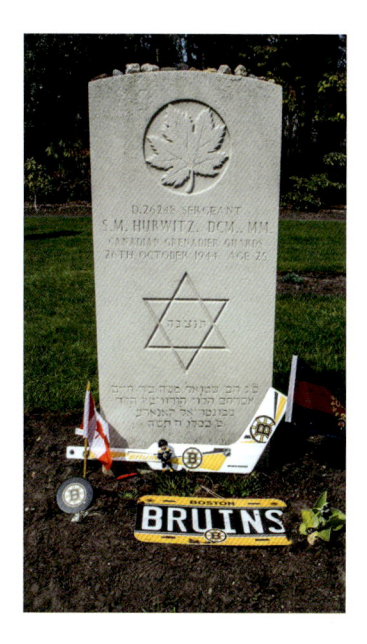

Bergen-Op-Zoom War Cemetery, The Netherlands. (2017) This grave made me smile. Perhaps Sgt. Hurwitz was a Boston Bruins fan! Even after all these years, his family has not forgotten that, bringing some memorabilia to place at his grave.

Ramparts Cemetery, Lille Gate, Ypres, Belgium. 127 burials (7 unidentified).[110] (2017)

[108] Commonwealth War Graves Commission. (n.d.). *Cemetery*. Retrieved from https://www.cwgc.org/find-a-cemetery/cemetery/66900/plugge's-plateau-cemetery,-anzac/
[109] Commonwealth War Graves Commission. (n.d.). *Search Results*. Retrieved from https://www.cwgc.org/search-results?term=tyne%2Bcot&name=tyne%2Bcot&fullname=tyne%2Bcot
[110] Commonwealth War Graves Commission. (n.d.). *Cemetery*. Retrieved from https://www.cwgc.org/find-a-cemetery/cemetery/51404/ramparts-cemetery,-lille-gate/

Chunuk Bair memorial and cemetery, Gallipoli, Turkey (2015). Author Rudyard Kipling was 'poet laureate' of what was then called the Imperial War Graves Commission (now the Commonwealth War Graves Commission). One of his jobs was to select the words used in the cemeteries and monuments such as "Their name liveth for evermore", "Known unto God" and "Lest we forget".

across the world – in more than 150 countries. Ten per cent of the Commission's budget comes from Canada.[111]

Walking through the acres of cemetery grounds not only provides visuals and individual names to the numbers, it gives you a sense of how different nations dealt with their own war dead.

The United States of America (through either intent or necessity) chose regional cemeteries. The American Battlefield Monuments Commission maintains a total of fifty-three World War I and World War II cemeteries and memorials in nineteen countries and territories, commemorating almost 220,000 fallen and missing.[112]

I find that the Commonwealth cemeteries feel cozy and peaceful – even the immense ones like Tyne Cot. The Normandy American

A British tank crew buried together in Hermanville War Cemetery, Sword Beach, Normandy, France. (2001)

---

[111] Commonwealth War Graves Commission. (2017). *Financial statements for the year ended 31 March 2017*. Maidenhead, United Kingdom.
[112] American Battle Monuments Commission. (n.d.). *Cemeteries & memorials | American Battle Monuments Commission*. Retrieved from https://abmc.gov/cemeteries-memorials

Cemetery, which I visited in 2001, felt large, substantial, impressive. Lines of white crosses stretched as far as I could see and the reflecting pool made everything feel even larger and more grand.

The German War Graves Commission (Volksbund) maintains 833 war cemeteries in forty-six countries, commemorating 2.7 million fallen and missing service members.[113] Despite the country's proximity to many of the battlefields, Germany chose to bury fallen service members on the battlefields instead of repatriating them. The country was not, however, awarded as much land for this purpose as the Allies, forcing them to do so using mass graves.

The Langemark cemetery in Flanders contains 44,292 burials. Approximately 25,000 of the burials are contained in a mass grave near the entrance to the cemetery. Their names are listed on black pillars surrounding the grave and a sculpture of four grieving figures watches over it. The rest of the burials are in smaller group graves of four to eight men.[114]

Normandy American Cemetery, Omaha Beach, Normandy, France. (2001)

As with a couple of other essays in this book, I wrote this in public, specifically in the kitchen of a hostel while I was out of town. As I wrote this section one morning, a couple of German men came in to make their breakfast. I struck up a conversation with one of them and asked him if, in his travels, he had ever visited any battlefields. He said 'no', which didn't really surprise me. I have not actually met too many fellow travellers who have also spent time on the battlefields. I think a lot of people are not interested or simply do not think about it because it all happened so long ago now. I hope this book will change a few people's minds.

---

[113] Volksbund. (n.d.) Uber uns. Retrieved from https://www.volksbund.de/en/presse/volksbund.html
[114] Holt, T., & Holt, V. (2008). *Major & Mrs. Holt's battlefield guide to the Ypres Salient & Passchendaele*. Barnsley: Pen & Sword Military. p. 135.

Remembering the Dead

My fellow hosteller told me that when he was in school in Germany, most of what he was taught centered on the Holocaust and when they did think about those who fell in the wars, it was more common to remember everyone who fell – military or civilian, no matter which side of the conflict they were on. I could not agree more. While this collection of essays focuses on Canadian sacrifices in the war, from a Canadian's perspective, we should never forget the other millions of lives changed by these wars and those that continue to be waged.

The French, it seems, also agree.

The mass grave at Langemark German Military Cemetery, Flanders, Belgium. The names of the 25,000 soldiers buried in this plot are listed on the black pillars along the sides of the grave. (2017)

Two British soldiers buried in the mass grave at Langemark German Military Cemetery. (2017)

Black crosses in German cemeteries are ornamental and do not necessarily indicate burials. Langemark German military cemetery, Belgium. (2017)

Smaller group graves throughout the Langemark German Military Cemetery, Belgium. (2017)

La Cambe German Military Cemetery contains 21,222 burials. The mound in the centre, topped with a sculpture of two figures and a cross, contains a mass burial of almost 300 soldiers, 207 of them unidentified.[115] (2001)

---

[115] Volksbund Deutsche Kriegsgräberfürsorge. (n.d.). *La Cambe (factsheet)*.

Remembering the Dead

The French War Graves Commission maintains 265 military cemeteries in France, the final resting place to 740,000 French service members and two thousand sites in seventy-eight other countries.[116] Notre Dame de Lorette, within sight of Vimy Ridge, is the largest French military cemetery with 39,985 burials and a small chapel. It was started in 1915 and grew as burials from smaller cemeteries were brought to this location.[117] It seemed to me like a mix of Commonwealth and American cemeteries – rows of crosses in a cozy setting. Across the road is the Ring of Remembrance.

Dedicated on Remembrance Day, 2014, the Ring of Remembrance is a monument to all the soldiers who fell in Northern France in World War I, alphabetically, with distinction between neither rank nor nationality. Both sides of the conflict are remembered side by side, Germans alongside British and French, with the 580,000 names etched into 500 long metal panels. It is the ultimate international memorial to the Great War. An enclosed ring, there is just one door and two small windows, one of which has a view of the Vimy Memorial in the distance.

Throughout the captions of cemetery photographs in this book, I included both the total number of burials and, when possible, the number of those burials only "Known Unto God". I like numbers and so included both of these statistics in the lectures I presented about the 2017 trip. After the first few presentations, I thought the unidentified number was not needed and considered removing that information. A discussion with a couple in the audience after my third lecture made me keep that information in the presentation and include them here.

The gentleman's father was buried in Europe, killed in World War II. His family had visited the grave a couple of times. After hearing the numbers of all the unidentified bodies, and of all the names on the walls with no known graves, they realized how lucky his family had been – to know what happened to his father, to have a

French military cemetery at Notre Dame de Lorette. (2017)

---

[116] Government of France. (n.d.). *Les sépultures de guerre*. (n.d.). Retrieved from https://www.defense.gouv.fr/memoire/memoire/sepultures-et-monuments-aux-morts/les-sepultures-de-guerre

[117] Ministry of Defence. (n.d.). *Notre-Dame-de-Lorette | Chemins de Mémoire - Ministère de la Défense*. Retrieved from http://www.cheminsdememoire.gouv.fr/en/notre-dame-de-lorette-0

142 Remembrance Road

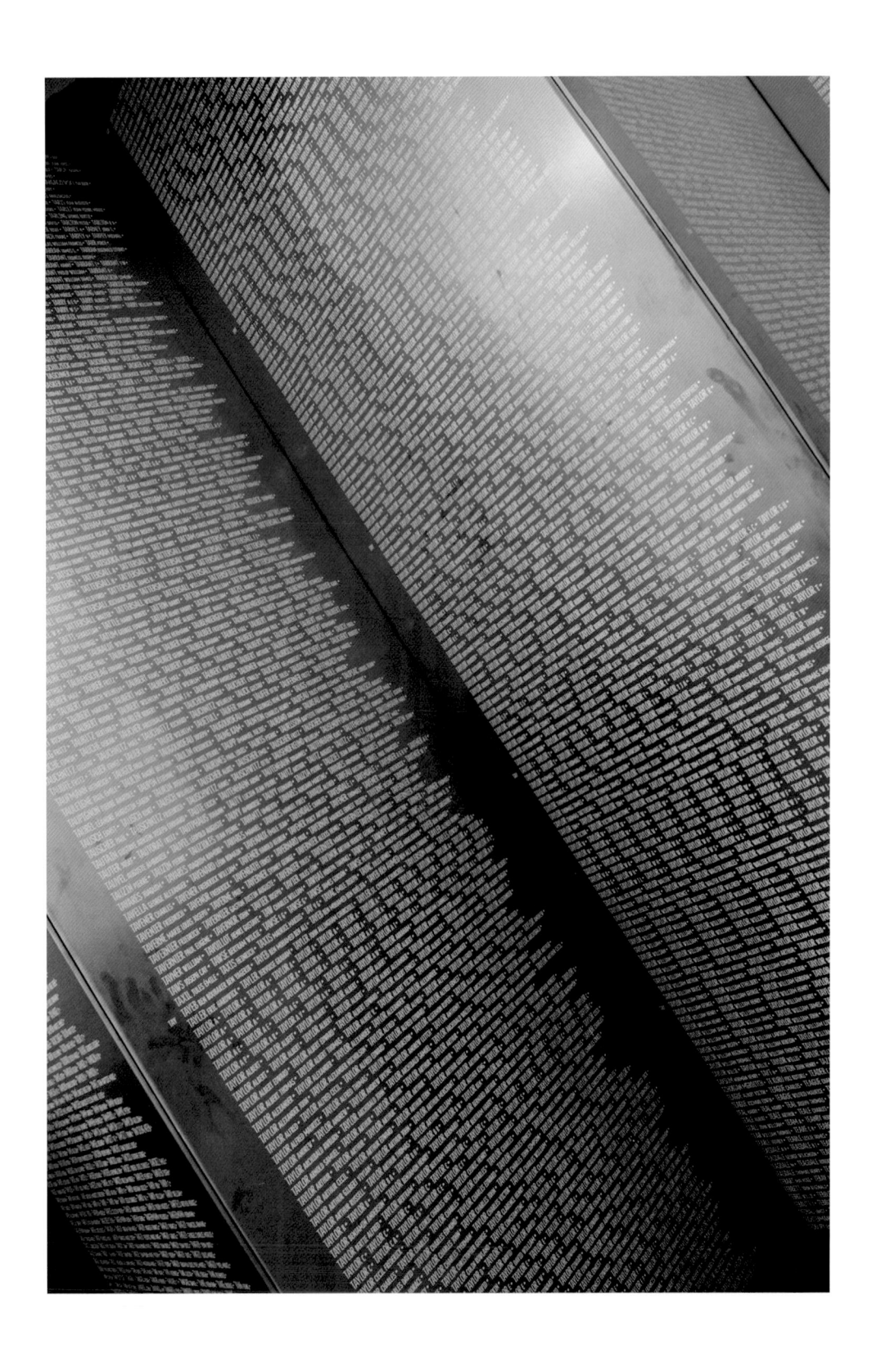

headstone and a plot of land they could visit, even if it was halfway around the world, unlike the families of those names on the walls and nameless bodies in the ground. Those families never knew what happened to their father or son or brother or husband. They never had that closure. All they had was a name etched into a tiny section of a wall in amongst the names of thousands of other men whose families also had no closure.

It is not practical for everyone to travel overseas to pay respects to our war dead. With Commonwealth War Graves in 154 countries, however, there are likely cemeteries and burials closer to home. The CWGC maintains an excellent online database of all sites, burials and memorials. You can visit their website (www.cwgc.org) and quickly research a family member or find a nearby location. It was an invaluable tool in preparation for my 2017 trip.

Ring of Remembrance, Notre Dame de Lorette, France. (2017)

Facing page: Ring of Remembrance, Notre Dame de Lorette, France. (2017) Seeing the tiny names filling this large memorial, knowing this is just a small sampling of the men who fell in the war, puts everything into sharp focus.

A small memorial left at the Ring of Remembrance. (2017)

145   Remembering the Dead

Get an idea of Canada's World War II preparations at home by exploring Fort Petrie in Cape Breton, Nova Scotia or even taking a tour of the Citadel in Halifax or other museums closer to you. Look out for lectures by veterans in your community.

It is important to learn about these wars and remember everyone who experienced war and consequently lost their lives, if we are to have any hope of avoiding the same mistakes in the future.

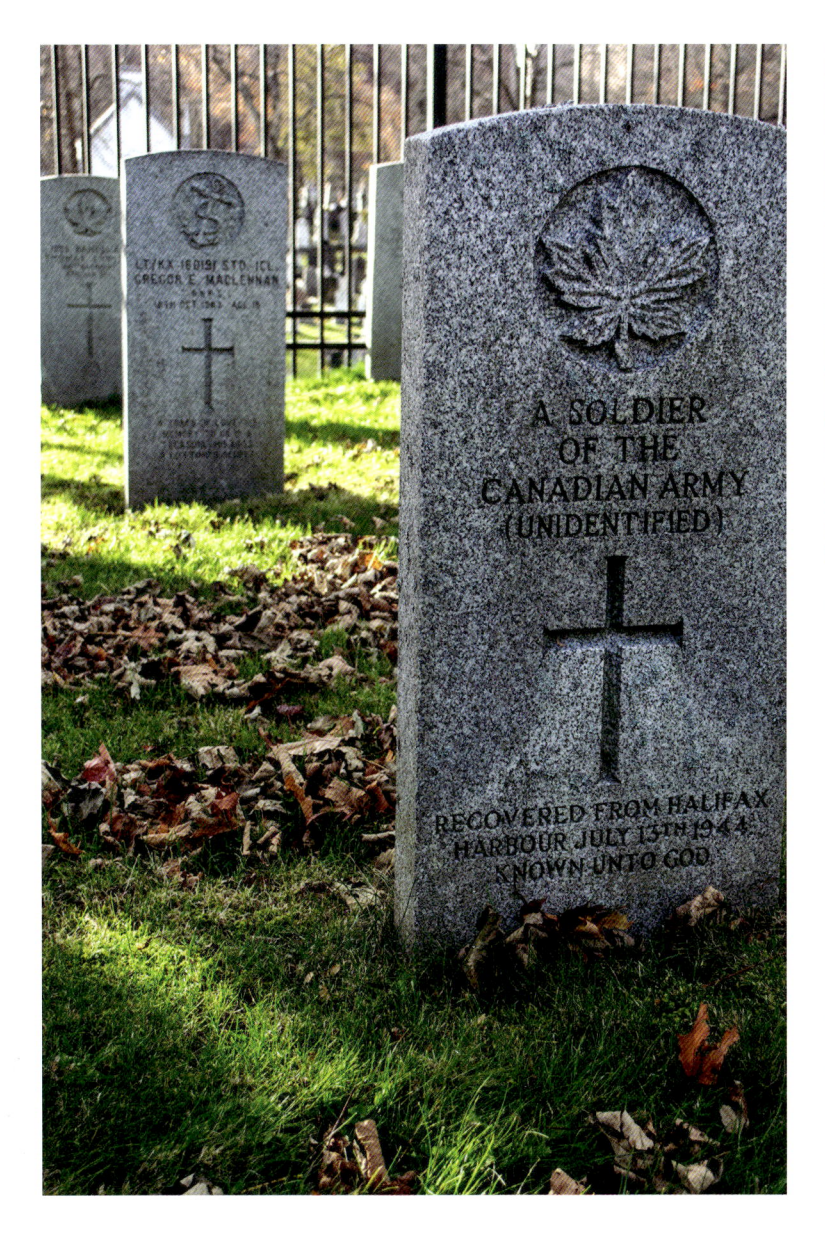

Fort Petrie, Cape Breton. Part of the Sydney Harbour fortifications. (2016).

An unidentified burial in Fort Massey Military Cemetery, Halifax, Nova Scotia. (2017)

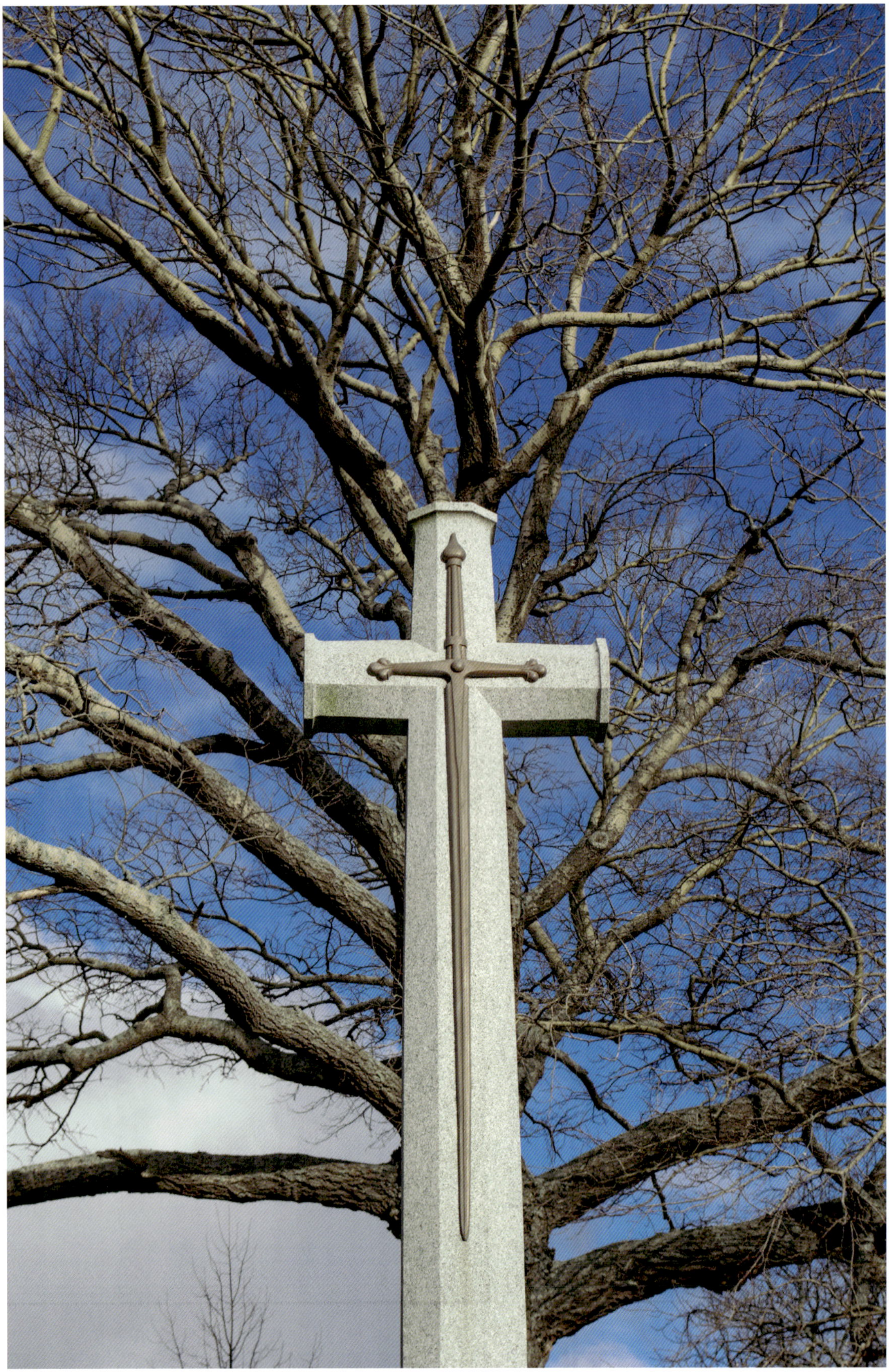

147   Remembering the Dead

The Halifax Citadel
National Historic Site
of Canada. (2017)

Facing page: Cross of Sacrifice, Fort Massey Military
Cemetery, Halifax, Nova Scotia. 128 burials.[118] (2017)

[118] Commonwealth War Graves Commission. (n.d.). *Cemetery*. Retrieved from https://www.cwgc.org/find-a-cemetery/cemetery/2103726/halifax-(fort-massey)-cemetery/

Gun keeping watch over the Dardanelles Narrows, Gallipoli Battlefield, Turkey. Part of the memorial at the Kilitbahir gun batteries. (2015)

Appendix One - Relevant Dates

Military Time Line

1914 – Start of World War I / First Battle of Ypres

1915 – Start of the Gallipoli campaign / Second Battle of Ypres

1916 – End of the Gallipoli campaign / Battle of the Somme

1917 – Battle of Vimy Ridge / Third Battle of Ypres (Passchendaele)

1918 – End of World War I

1939 – Start of World War II

1940 – Dunkirk Evacuation

1942 – Dieppe Raid

1944 – D-Day (Operation Overlord/Invasion of Normandy) / Operation Market Garden / Battle of the Scheldt / Battle of Geilenkirchen

1945 – Liberation of Dachau and Auschwitz Concentration Camps Liberation of The Netherlands / End of World War II

Personal Time Line

1997 – Moved to Europe

1998 – Visited Vimy Ridge / Attended my first Nijmegen Victory March / Visited Cyprus and Israel

1999 – Nijmegen Victory March

2000 – Visited Dachau Concentration Camp

2001 – Battlefield Tour including: Palace of Versailles, Flanders, Normandy, Dieppe, Dunkirk / Returned to Canada

2015 – Visited Gallipoli, Turkey

2017 – Battlefield Tour including: Vimy 100 ceremony, Normandy, Dieppe, The Somme, Flanders, Auschwtiz

Bibliography and Resources

Books

Barris, T. (2004). *Juno: Canadians at D-Day, June 6, 1944*. Toronto: Allen.

Beevor, A. (2014). *D-day: The battle for Normandy*. London: Penguin Books, p. 131.

Berton, P. (1986). *Vimy*. Toronto: McClelland and Stewart.

Betts, A. (Ed.), *In Flanders Fields: 100 years* Canada: Knopf.

Black, D., & Boileau, J. (2015). *Old enough to fight: Canada's boy soldiers in the First World War*. Toronto: James Lorimer & Company.

Dann, S. (1998). *Dachau 29 April 1945: TherRainbow liberation memoirs*. Lubbock, TX: Texas Tech University Press.

Desquesnes, R. (1989). *The landing beaches*. Editions Ouest-France, p. 15.

Erickson, E. J. (2010). *Gallipoli: The ottoman campaign*. Barnsley: Pen & Sword Military.

Ford, K. (1994). *Assault on Germany: The battle for Geilenkirchen*. Southampton, England: Valda Books.

Gilbert, M. (2007). *The battle of the Somme: The heroism and horror of war*. Toronto: McClelland & Stewart.

Gogos, F. (2015). *The Royal Newfoundland Regiment in the Great War: A guide to the battlefields and memorials of France, Belgium, and Gallipoli*. St. John's : Flanker Press Limited.

Hart, P. (2011). *Gallipoli*. Oxford University Press.

Holt, T., & Holt, V. (2014). *Major & Mrs. Holt's battlefield guide to the Ypres Salient & Passchendaele*. Barnsley: Pen & Sword Military.

Humphreys, E. (2014). *Great Canadian battles*. London, United Kingdom: Arcturus.

Kemp, A. (n.d.). *Pegasus Bridge - The first British assault*. Caen: Èditions Memorial, p. 4.

Longworth, P. (2003). *The unending vigil: A history of the Commonwealth War Graves Commission*. Barnsley, S. Yorkshire: Leo Cooper.

McKay, J. P., Buckler, J., & Hill, B. D. (2001). *A history of western society*. Boston: Houghton Mifflin.

Nicholson, G. W. L. (2007). *The fighting Newfoundlander*. Montréal, Québec: McGill-Queen's University Press.

Raddall, T. H. (2014). *West Novas: A history of the West Nova Scotia Regiment*. Halifax, Nova Scotia: Dalhousie University.

Ryan, C. (2007). *A bridge too far*. London: Hodder.

Shay, J. (2002). *Odysseus in America: Combat trauma and the trials of homecoming*. New York: Scribner.

Tennyson, B. D. (2017). *Nova Scotia at war, 1914-1919*. Toronto: Nimbus Publishing, Limited.

Uttridge, S., & Catton, C. (2014). *The encyclopaedia of warfare*. London: Amber Books.

Veranov, M. (2010). *The Third Reich at war*. London: Magpie Books.

Webster, D. (1998). *Aftermath: The remnants of war*. New York: Vintage Books.

Web and Additional Resources

American Battle Monuments Commission – abmc.gov

Commonwealth War Graves Commission – www.cwgc.org/– Genealogical, military, and cemetery research

Dan Carlin's Hardcore History - www.dancarlin.com/hardcore-history-series/ - An amazing, in-depth history podcast, including at least fifteen hours of content on World War I.

Legion Canada's Military History Magazine - legionmagazine.com

Living History with Mat McLachlan – www.battlefields.com.au – A great podcast focused on Australian military history.

Royal Canadian Air Force - www.rcaf-arc.forces.gc.ca – Aircraft descriptions and history.

Veterans Affairs Canada - www.veterans.gc.ca - Educational resources

Acknowledgements

There are many people I need to thank for making this book possible. I'll start with my family - so thanks to my parents for all the opportunities they've give me through the years and, with my brother, all the support and encouragement they've given me regarding my photography and writing. I'd also like to gratefully acknowledge the Canadian Armed Forces for giving our family many of the opportunities we've had.

While we spent a lot of time exploring battlefields just as a family, many of my experiences would not have been possible without the help of others. The staff of the Personnel Support Programs in Niederheid, Germany arranged so many great excursions and trips, whether we enjoyed the sun in Spain or learned some history on the way to the Nijmegen Victory March. Thanks to Shari, my travel agent, for finding such amazing and meaningful tours in Western Europe and Gallipoli, Turkey.

Thank you to my Turkish guides, with Crowded House tours, Ecebat, whose names I can't remember but who gave me so much excellent information in Gallipoli; to Paola, our GoAhead tour guide in charge of wrangling all of us during our ten day Vimy 100 tour, sharing her stories and encouraging us to share our own. Finally, thank you to my aunt Donna for putting up with me during the trip, my debatable navigation skills and our shared plague notwithstanding.

I can't thank Bria and Kate at the Kings County Museum, in Kentville, N.S. enough. Thank you for believing in this project and agreeing to host my exhibit even before I left for the 2017 trip and taken the photos. Also to Carly at NSCC Institute of Technology Campus, Halifax, N.S. for hosting an exhibit there as well. Another special thank you to Kate for connecting me to Scott Smith at SSP Publications. Without you showing him my little scrapbook, this book would not have happened.

Speaking of which... thanks to Scott for seeing potential in that scrapbook and thinking it was something worth expanding and

Acknowledgements

publishing, even when I didn't, and to his team for turning my random words and pictures into something great. Christina and Tanya at Veterans Affairs Canada, Danny at the Royal Canadian Legion and Carrie at Visual Arts Nova Scotia were all so helpful in answering my questions.

A big thank you to everyone who suffered through my drafts so that it read well and the information was accurate – Donna, Kathy and Lana; Craig Roach not only worked with Shari to arrange my tour of Gallipoli, but checked my facts in some of these essays. Of course, the authors and editors of all the books and resources I referenced were so helpful.

For all their support and encouragement through the years: thanks to Courtney, Lana, Re, Shelley, Stacey, the Bestword writing group, Kings County Photography Club and my photo buddies, A. Main and Debbie.

Finally, and most importantly, thank you to our service men and women, past and present, who have served and sacrificed for our country.

~ Justine

Spanish poppy fields.
(2000)

Small memorials left around the trenches of the Sanctuary Wood Museum, in Flanders. (2017)

About the Author

Justine MacDonald is a travel photographer and blogger based in Nova Scotia's Annapolis Valley. She loves exploring history, and the world in general, through the lens of her camera.

She enjoys sharing her knowledge and love of photography with others – to inspire them to see the world in a new light – through introductory workshops, one-on-one tutorials, photo walks and travel presentations. She is the official photographer for *Broken Leg Theatre* (a variety show produced in Wolfville, N.S. three times a year) and sells her work through online shops and subscriptions.

An award-winning photographer, she has participated in several group and solo exhibitions. You can find her work online at www.justinemacdonald.photography.

Photo: Kimberley Peterson-Kuhn, Kulusuk, Greenland. (2007)

Notes